Finding the Charm in Charm City

Finding the

CHARM IN CHARM CITY
Affectionate Views of BALTIMORE

Photographs by
HUGUETTE D. MAY

Text by
ANTHEA SMITH

With a Foreword by Michael Olesker

THE JOHNS HOPKINS UNIVERSITY PRESS   *Baltimore & London*

The Johns Hopkins University Press
2715 North Charles Street
Baltimore, Maryland 21218-4363
www.press.jhu.edu

Library of Congress Cataloging-in-Publication Data will be found at the end of this book.
A catalog record for this book is available from the British Library.

ISBN 0-8018-5929-8

Contents

Foreword

Ours is an age of homogenization. The little neighborhood grocery store yields to the McDonald's serving eighty billion cheeseburgers with a side order of angioplasty. The councilman who once kept dice in his City Hall desk in case a game of craps happened to break out gives way to the silky politician who dresses like a TV anchorman and talks like a tax accountant. The past goes thataway.

Photographs are messages each generation sends to the future: This is what it was like before you got here—and, boy, did you miss something swell. In Baltimore, the tourists may arrive seeking Harborplace, but the smart ones stick around long enough to notice the edges of things: Fells Point's cobblestones, trod upon by generations of hucksters hustling fruits and vegetables with what Mencken called "lubricious gloats and gurgles"; the way the light falls in a West Baltimore churchyard; a South Street eatery that looks like a Hopper painting sprung to life; the way blue-grey formstone covers miles of rowhouses, prompting a former Peale Museum director to call it "the Berlin Wall with windows."

As Huguette May and Anthea Smith look about, they wonder "why some people had the sense to leave good things alone." We're a throwaway society. Most of us, putterers and builders-up and breakers-down, tend to potchke with things. We grow restless, we look to cash in, we move about. We grow bored and we change things. In our ever-diminishing attention spans, we seek new amusements. And then we mourn what we've lost. May and Smith are enthusiastic tour guides to Baltimore's nooks and crannies, plenty of them bound, inevitably, for the attic places of our collective psyches, where we'll lament their loss in years to come.

A few decades ago, somebody noticed Baltimore enjoying a renaissance and decided we needed a name. *Charm City* was invented. Some of the old-timers cringed at the notion, thinking it sounded like a Chamber of Commerce brainstorm. The city was too idiosyncratic for such a title, too willfully out of step with things. Remember, we're the place that gave John Waters his grand vision. We're upscale Washington's wayward Brooklyn. We're the town where the (rare) tourists used to say, "I'll take a sleeping pill to make sure I can keep up with the pace."

But the name has stuck because charm comes in many forms. We can love the annual Flower Mart at Mount Vernon but still admit there's also room for that big papier-mâché gorilla head near the Hollins Market. We've got the grandest collection of sixteenth-century paintings at the Walters, but there's also room for the beer can art of Federal Hill and the happy tin man overlooking Kelly's Weld Um-Up on Ritchie Highway. Maybe there's charm in the nightly reveling at Oriole Park at Camden Yards, but we also remember the old girl on Thirty-third Street, Memorial Stadium, as the wrecking ball prepares to do its damnable work.

May and Smith hold onto it all for a little longer. One of the delights of this book is the offbeat history it offers. They recall, for example, the postwar fight over a name for the former home of the Orioles and the Colts. Babe Ruth Field, some wanted. Just a moment, said some cranky Gold Star Mothers, this stadium was supposed to memorialize the nation's war dead, and never mind some famous ballplayer, even if he was Baltimore's Babe. So the armies of Ruth backed down.

While treasuring our idiosyncracies, Baltimoreans have the happy facility for simultaneously laughing at some of them. We get the jokes. Nobody has to nudge us in the ribs when the sign at Hub Cap City on Belair Road advertises, "Don't go around with your lug nuts showing." We know that the little garden on Lake Avenue, with its bushes and shrubs sculpted into various animals, ain't exactly the gardens at Versailles, but we appreciate the twinkle in the eye behind its modest reach. We know that some people go to the Mechanic and the Lyric but, hey, hon, how about how the sun used to set so nice behind the old McCormick's spice plant on Light Street?

Art's in the eye of the beholder. Bob Blatchley, former newspaper reporter, former radio newsman, now an attorney for Baltimore Gas and Electric, likes to tell people, "I grew up on lower Greenmount Avenue, but now I notice it's become an artist's colony. Almost every week, the cops come down and draw a chalk outline of some guy's body on the sidewalk."

That's a Baltimore lifer laughing mordantly at the change of things. Photographs let us hold onto yesterday a little longer. Blatchley once worked at a newspaper called the *News American*, at Lombard and South Streets. When the paper died in the mid-1980s, the old building was torn down and turned into that ubiquitous modern triumph, the parking lot.

America tends to reinvent itself a lot. This is refreshing, and keeps us from going stale, but allows us no pilgrimage to the things that came before us. We lose a sense of continuity when buildings full of character yield to parking lots full of nothing but the profit motive. We lose a sense of our uniqueness when we give up an old Calvert Street federal courthouse, with its history (Spiro Agnew copped his famous plea there) and its dark architectural spirit, for the new Lombard Street federal courthouse, which looks like nothing so much as a multilevel parking garage.

The best of Baltimore's photographic charms have always had some age on them; like some wizened old lady, they've sloughed off the last of any self-consciousness. It's Bolton Hill posing for a picture postcard on a frosty night, or the painted window screens of Highlandtown, or all those aluminum beach chairs with the plastic webbing and the bony arthritic knees coming out of them on the pavements of Fort Avenue on summer evenings.

Anthea Smith writes about the character of things,

knowing full well that character isn't something that comes in a can. It arrives slowly, and with age, and with the daily wear and tear that finally becomes a history.

Those of us who have been here a while will inevitably connect our own lives with some of Huguette May's photos. That snowball stand: How many times did kids in the old neighborhood cool off on airless August nights with one of those icy delights?

Or the coffee sign at Funk's: Isn't that the place about which the late City Councilman Mimi DiPietro, maestro of the malaprop, once declared, "They got the best coffee in town. They must have them coffee urinals going day and night."

Or the Apollo movie theater on Harford Road below North Avenue: In my youth, I spent glorious Saturday afternoons there, watching weekly adventure serials, cartoons galore, Movietone News, Previews of Coming Attractions, and double features to carry my imagination through the week.

May and Smith show us what's become of the Apollo in its old age. It's a nice little history, to which I'll add a piece of my own. A few years ago, covering some problem on Harford Road, I found myself standing under the old Apollo marquee when a young neighborhood kid approached me.

"Paper?" he asked, seeming to recognize my features.

I figured he knew me from my picture in the *Baltimore Sun* newspaper. Here was true recognition, the prodigal son returned home to the embrace of a brand new generation in his old neighborhood.

"Sunpaper?" I said.

"Sunpaper?" the kid repeated. "Sheet. I'm talking about reefer paper."

It's God who's in the details, but sometimes it's the devil, too. A building's just a building until you connect it to a little unanticipated history. Like Baltimore itself, this book's a collection of offbeat, quirky, often unnoticed charms. Smith's words are our pilgrimage to yesterday. May's photos are Bawlamorese for the eyes.

Michael Olesker

Preface

I'm a photographer and an artist. I've spent my life looking at things and asking questions. What is it made of? How does the light play across it at different times of the day or year? Is it a one-of-a-kind building and unique in its form? How has aging enhanced it? What is its character? But it took a chance occurrence with my retired neighbor to show me how little of Baltimore I had actually "seen" in my ten years as a city resident.

On a chilly morning in the fall of 1995, George called to ask me for a lift to his childhood neighborhood. I had certainly heard of Highlandtown, but before his call for a ride, I'd never had a reason to go there. We left Parkville and headed down Belair Road for a few miles, turning left onto Erdman Avenue, then right on Edison Highway. As we entered Highlandtown at Monument Street, a splash of red paint and gleaming glass block caught my eye. The classic art deco design of the long vacant Luby's Chevrolet building, looking forlorn amid weedy cracked sidewalks, invited me to come closer and explore its faded beauty. Of course, I could not stop then, but I knew I had to return soon with my camera. Too often, the opportunity to capture a unique image can slip away, and I was determined not to let that happen.

Another turn found us on streets with tidy rowhouses in the residential heart of Highlandtown. I quickly noticed the black and green vitrine tile exterior of Elberth's Meats, then the large octagonal front window and shiny emerald door of O'Donnell's Pub, and finally the mysterious Ducky Pleasure Club, its name spelled out in tiny dark blue ceramic tiles. If this one local neighborhood had these streetside gems, how many other such places were unknown to me? My guess was

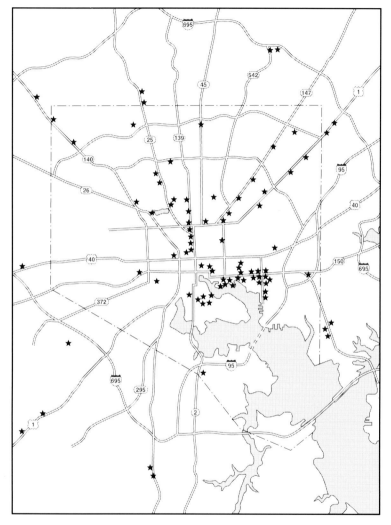

A few of the charming spots in Baltimore—all of them highlighted in the following pages.

dozens, perhaps hundreds, throughout the city. But why do I call them gems? Because they're precious and brighten our lives with grace and beauty and humor, adding luster to modern life, made bleak, as it is, by the stark new buildings and slick plastic signs of urban renewal. Thanks to George, I couldn't wait to get back to my studio and start planning how best to record my new discoveries.

With my eyes newly opened, I wanted to find and record the many other places around Baltimore which had retained their special character—not only for me but for others who would never travel these roads so near and yet so far away. But how would I go about finding them? I knew I needed a methodical approach to have the best chance of exploring the many sections of the city. Looking at a large map, I realized that Baltimore has major corridors along which I could easily travel. Map pins could mark the locations of each subject and show me at a glance whether there were areas I had missed, an especially helpful approach, as many of these locales were not well known to me.

The fun of a project such as this was that familiar parts of town now took on a new appeal. Wherever I went, I noticed Baltimore's distinctive details, the texture of the city with its varieties of Formstone; colorful murals new and old; stained-glass doorway transoms; fanciful screen paintings; hand-lettered signs of old pubs, warehouses, and eateries; and imaginatively decorated front yards complete with statues of the Virgin, ceramic animals, and festive flowers. The seemingly mundane became quite beautiful in varying kinds of light.

As I framed my subjects through the camera lens—a bright pink turret rising against a blue sky, a wall of yellow bricks raked with sunlight and shadows, or a vintage movie theater at dusk—I wondered why some people had the sense to leave good things alone. Was it by accident, benign neglect, or a conscious decision? Whatever the answer, I was amazed and glad that they had.

These pages represent my version of a visual "Balmorese" that celebrates the unique, the forgotten, the quirky, the hidden, the well-loved—streetside charms that are, or were, special to this city because they are either duplicated in no other place or we have adopted them as our own. Regrettably, it's already too late for the White Tower restaurant on Erdman Avenue, which I captured only three weeks before its demise. All that remains is a lonely looking plain white building with dusty outlines where its familiar lettering used to be.

H. M.

I am a writer and a painter but, more important to this book, I am also a person with a very inquisitive mind. I want to know about people, places, and things. Who were they? Where were they from? Why did they do what they did? Why did they settle here? When Huguette laid out the photographs she wanted to include in this book, I quickly realized there were many parts of Baltimore that I knew little or nothing about, even though I've spent most of my adult life here, and that my job would be to find out the stories behind the images.

My first step was to determine the exact location of each of the subjects, then determine which of the businesses were still in operation. Armed with my master list, I felt like a private eye searching for missing persons, especially when there was no apparent way to document some of the older, now defunct businesses. I've always loved libraries and the wealth of knowledge they contain, so one of my first stops was the Maryland Room of the Enoch Pratt Free Library. Many of my days were spent looking through their valuable files of early newspaper and magazine accounts for any shred of information that would help me in my quest. I also looked through biographical files and obituaries, hoping to discover names that were connected to the topics in question.

Besides the individual locations that were photographed, the history of each road that served as an organizing corridor had to be included, and that involved more searching for the origins of our state's system of roads and highways. My stack of notes grew larger.

Some stories seemed to defy discovery, but I refused to be defeated. I talked to anyone who would listen, drove to where the buildings were located and knocked on doors, and looked in the phone book for people with the same last name as that of the business in question. One such call was to Gertrude Elberth, who lived near Elberth's Meats, a business about which I had been unable to glean any information. This kind and gracious woman turned out to be the granddaughter of the founder, and, when I explained what I was doing, she told me the whole story of the various family businesses and of life in her little section of the city. A similar conversation took place with octogenarian August Nolte, whose whole working life has been involved with movie theaters, several of which are included here.

Then there were the serendipitous connections that occurred. Early on, I was having a conversation with my travel agent when she told me about her husband's new design studio in a great old building at Toone and Bayliss Streets in Canton. Knowing that this was the same location as one of the buildings I was desperately searching for, I asked if it might be the Atlantic Southwestern Broom Company building, and she said it was. A call to her husband gave me the phone number of Scott Rosenberger, the founder's great-grandson, who still owns the property even though the broom business was sold years ago.

Other subjects, such as the "Vote against Prohibition" sign in Fells Point, required finding out the history of life in our city during those turbulent years. Or the early Coca-Cola sign painted on a building on North Avenue. What was the significance of Coca-Cola in Baltimore? I made more trips to the Maryland Room files to find anything related to these subjects.

As I discovered each scrap of information, I became more excited and pressed harder to find out even more. Friends and family listened patiently as I recited my latest findings, bubbling over with facts, figures, and anecdotes about each and every subject included in the book.

In the end, there were some places that needed only a brief description. But for other locations, and the neighborhoods in which they reside, I hope that you will be enriched by what I have been able to tell you. To me, such knowledge makes life in our city so much more interesting.

A. S.

As Baltimore looks ahead to the twenty-first century, perhaps we can pause here to remember and enjoy the vitality of a city that has retained so much of its neighborly charm, thanks to the devotion and dedication of countless unnamed individuals who have made it their business to lavish care and affection on their particular areas of the city. Whether you are new to Baltimore or have lived here all of your life, we invite you to join us in exploring these lesser-known sites that truly make Baltimore "Charm City."

Acknowledgments

The journey this project took me on would not have been possible without the enthusiastic participation of a number of people. I wish to thank Anthea Smith, artist and Renaissance woman, for saying yes when I asked if she would consider writing words to accompany my images, for applying her considerable writing, organizational, and research skills so adeptly to a most challenging variety of imagery, for her astonishing patience, and most of all, for her friendship; Bert Smith, for his belief that in my first five images was the germ of a worthwhile project, for his encouragement to develop that project into a full-fledged book, and for his numerous suggestions and unqualified enthusiasm for my work; Brenda Ruby, who prepared the initial presentation; and Robert J. Brugger at the Johns Hopkins University Press for his vision in helping this book evolve to its present form, for guiding the project through the labyrinthine process of approvals and funding, for sharing my belief that Baltimore deserves a closer look, and for trusting that I could deliver.

Special thanks go to George and Frances Rott, who, for my eleven years in Baltimore, could not have been kinder or more generous neighbors; Tom Kiefaber, for granting permission to include the essential Senator Theatre in this book; John and Pat Gidwitz and Linda and Harry Moxley, who, despite their own hectic schedules, graciously provided the comfort of their homes during some of my weekend shoots in Baltimore; Anne Didush Schuler and Hans Schuler at the Schuler School of Fine Arts, for providing a pivotal and unforgettable learning experience during my early days in Baltimore; Dr. Bruce Rosenblum, for his advice and support; Roy Sparks and Penny Jung, my mentors at Dundalk Community College, both of whom assured me upon graduation that I would succeed at whatever I did; Chris Powell, Judy Stoffer, and Ann Zaiman, who were always ready to share their insights and who have always understood and supported my aspirations; and my son, Noah May, who made each visit back to Baltimore extra special and who came through at the airport when most needed.

Most especially, thanks to my husband, Tom, without whose loving and absolute support in all aspects of my life this book would not exist and whose companionship, patience, humor, and navigational skills during many a photography sojourn for this project made a formidable task both manageable and fun.

And finally, thanks to the many Baltimoreans who wondered what that lady standing in the street with the camera was up to.

H. M.

My part in this project would not have been possible without the help and support of many people. First and foremost, my thanks go to Huguette May, for trusting me to research and write about her beautiful images. Thanks also to the staff of the Maryland Room of the Enoch Pratt Free Library; Anne Calhoun of the Perkins Library at the B & O Railroad Museum; the staff of the Dundalk Patapsco Neck Historical Society; Robert K. Headley Jr., for his vast store of information on the movie theaters of Baltimore; William A. Murray, for his profiles of Baltimore's firefighters; Jacques Kelly, for his descriptions of Charles Village; Gary Kachadourian, with the Mayor's Advisory Committee on Art and Culture; Kathy Kotarba, with the Commission for Historical and Architectural Preservation; and Michael Galitzin, who answered my call to be a research assistant when time was short.

Special thanks go to the lengthy list of people who unselfishly shared a part of their lives with me, even though they had never met me before. Without each of you, there would be no words for this book.

Thanks to the people at the Johns Hopkins University Press for their professional skills, especially my manuscript editor, Celestia Ward, for her meticulous attention and encouraging support; Wilma Rosenberger, for her thoughtful and elegant design; and Robert J. Brugger, who had faith in my ability to write.

Last but not least, my deepest thanks go to the one person who listened to all my stories—my best friend and husband, Bert.

A.S.

Finding the Charm in Charm City

ONE

Route 2: Hanover Street/ Governor Ritchie Highway

Route 2 begins as Hanover Street near Baltimore's Inner Harbor. The name reportedly comes from the province in Germany where four different kings of England were born, all named George. Hanover Street then proceeds south through Port Covington, across the Middle Branch of the Patapsco River, then through the Cherry Hill neighborhood to the Interstate 895 interchange, where its name changes to the Governor Ritchie Highway, Maryland's first dual-lane high-speed road. Its namesake, Governor Albert Cabell Ritchie (1876–1936), served four terms as governor of Maryland, from 1920 to 1935.

When planned in the early 1930s, this highway was intended as a beautiful ceremonial boulevard stretching between Baltimore and Annapolis, similar in feel to the more serene Baltimore-Washington Parkway that lies to its west. However, in an effort to gain the necessary land inexpensively, promises of development were made to the owners of abutting properties, and commercial enterprises soon flourished, leaving today's Ritchie Highway a far cry from the intentions of its original planners.

For more than half of the company's sixty years, this painted sign at the corner of Cross and Leadenhall Streets has informed residents and visitors alike of ABC Box Company's business while treating them to a classic study in perspective. Though softened by over thirty years of exposure to the elements, the red background successfully continues to set off the sign painter's simple but dramatic two-dimensional rendering of a box viewed from above with all flaps open. A quick glance gives all the necessary information about this company, and the sign adds character to an otherwise plain brick wall.

A few blocks to the east on a nearby Federal Hill street, neighbors and passersby alike are treated to this window world of a man who is dedicated to his art—beer can art, that is, with Bud Light cans as the preferred medium. This artist's attention to detail, which makes his creations so rich, is immediately evident when one closely examines "Lumb's Diner," where tiny pots and pans hang inside and silver glitter enhances the sign. Appropriately in this port city, the diner shares its exhibition space with a sailing ship. A brief conversation with a passing neighbor reveals that there is an entire collection of related objects adorning the front of the artist's automobile, which seems likely to bring attention to itself wherever it goes.

Farther east of Hanover Street on Key Highway is the Baltimore Museum of Industry, which opened in November 1981 and is dedicated to the "art of work." Inside the walls of these beautifully restored buildings is the area's only working collection of factory and port relics dating from the industrial age of America (1830–1950). The buildings themselves date from the 1860s, when they served as a soda straw factory and oyster cannery.

Among the many fine examples of this earlier age is the automatic typesetting machine invented in a tiny office in East Baltimore by German immigrant Ottmar Merganthaler. The linotype revolutionized the setting of type for printing because it set an entire line of type at a time, hence its name. Also known as "hot type" because it uses molten lead to form the characters, the linotype represents an important step along the path from setting type laboriously by hand, one character at a time, to today's high-speed computerized methods.

Visitors will also discover a re-created antique machine shop, a clothing factory and garment loft, a shipbuilding and port machine shop, a food-processing plant, and a broadcasting and communications exhibit, as well as displays of Baltimore's past and present industries.

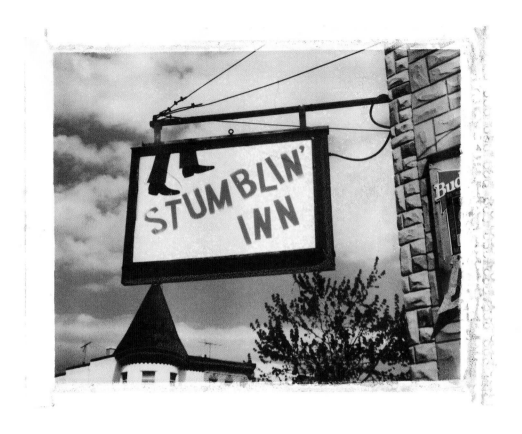

Local residents and workers at the nearby piers have enjoyed stopping by the small neighborhood bar on this corner in Locust Point since the mid-1960s. In true Baltimore fashion, Formstone covers its exterior. Originally known as the Driftwood Inn, the bar was sold in the late 1980s, and its present owner exhibited something of a sense of humor when he renamed it.

In a city that is so intimately connected with the flag, this patriotic window display prepared by the Ladies' Auxiliary of American Legion Post 133 in the heart of South Baltimore comes as no surprise. The founding of the American Legion, in March 1919, followed many often-stormy meetings of a great caucus at the Cirque de Paris, which drew a thousand officers and enlisted men representing the American Expeditionary Forces. The newly formed American Legion issued a charter to Maryland, one of the leading states in its formation, on May 24, 1919. The organization's founding principles include "making right the master of might."

Founded only twenty years later, the Fort McHenry Post began its service on Hull Street in Locust Point and moved to its present location on Fort Avenue in 1963. In addition to serving the interests of veterans, its more than 220 members are active in many programs that help with child welfare. Annual New Year's Eve and Halloween parties benefit the organization's causes, allowing post members to delight children with Easter baskets and regularly prepare baskets of food for those in need.

The beautifully carved keystone of this firehouse at Hanover and Ostend Streets portrays a typical firefighter of the late nineteenth century. The two-story red brick station of the Hook and Ladder Company 6 was dedicated on April 6, 1888, and remains in service today.

The paid fire department was only thirty years old when this firehouse opened. Before that time, firefighting was a volunteer effort. Although the first recorded fire in Baltimore City was in 1749, citizens did not establish any type of fire company until 1763 when they formed the Mechanical Fire Company, which served the city's needs for almost twenty years. Eight new companies, mainly bucket brigades, were formed from 1782 to 1805 to handle the rapid growth in town. With the development of riveted leather hose that could be connected to a nozzle, thirteen new hose companies were formed from 1810 to 1856.

In response to the need for coordination between the various volunteer fire companies, a convention of delegates met in 1834 and organized the Baltimore United Fire Department. Rules of response and identification were adopted, but intense rivalries remained between the companies. A disagreement over the ownership of horses sparked the riot in October 1858 that finally prompted the City Council to pass the ordinance that established the paid fire department.

South of the city on the Ritchie Highway section of Route 2 stands this unique and happy tin man, who has been welcoming customers of this welding shop in the Brooklyn area for the past six or seven years. His uplifting features were fashioned by a former customer who found himself in debt to the shop. The owner decided to accept the tin man as payment and promptly perched him high atop the shop to beckon customers in need of welding services. In this day of laundromats and automatic dryers, a source for custom-made clothesline poles provides a refreshing reminder of the labors of washdays long past, when clothes were actually hung outside to dry.

TWO

The Old Baltimore– Annapolis Road

The full length of today's route for the old Baltimore-Annapolis Road is almost unrecognizable for two reasons. First, much of the original road from Glen Burnie south has been absorbed by other highways. Second, the current Baltimore-Annapolis Road south of Glen Burnie, which parallels Ritchie Highway, was not created until 1915. The original highway, which predates the Revolutionary War, served as a major postal route between the north and south.

Beginning at Russell Street to the west of the Middle Branch in Baltimore, the old Baltimore-Annapolis Road travels south over the Patapsco River through the Lansdowne, Pumphrey, and Ferndale communities to Glen Burnie. Here the original road has been absorbed by Interstate 97, and the modern Baltimore-Annapolis Road veers off to the east as Maryland Route 648. At the lower end of this section, the old road crosses the Severn Run, following the divide between the Severn and South Rivers as it continues southeast to Annapolis. By choosing this route, the road's builders avoided having to cross the Severn River. This section gained the name *General's Highway* in 1783,

when George Washington used it to travel to Annapolis to resign his commission as commander-in-chief of the Continental Army. On that occasion, a reception committee from Annapolis traveled to meet him where General's Highway now meets U.S. Route 50.

Because the soil along the route offered little to attract big planters, the old road provided few comforts to the traveler, regardless of his stature in the community. South of the Severn Run, one could stop in at the Widow Ramsey's Tavern or

Several miles south of Baltimore, in the Ferndale neighborhood, musical albums from an earlier time beckon to observers from this simply designed window display. While compact discs may be the musical wave of the present and future, some people still desire the original $33\frac{1}{3}$ RPM long playing (LP) and 45 RPM records. So, for the past twenty-four years (nineteen at this location), happy hunters of jazz, blues, and rock-'n'-roll who hold fast to the platters of the past have often found their hearts' desires in this store.

try the Rising Sun Inn a few miles further south. Closer to Annapolis was Belvoir Manor, the home of John Ross, the great-grandfather of Francis Scott Key.

Despite its lack of amenities, the old Baltimore-Annapolis Road remained an important highway throughout the nineteenth century, and it continues to serve the area today in its various new configurations.

Puddles from a recent shower reflect the various angles of this snowball stand, located a few miles farther south of the city. Here the hot and thirsty traveler can find relief on a scorching summer day by indulging in one of the icy treats. While other stands may attract customers with garishly painted signs complete with palm trees or bottles of brightly colored sugar syrup, this one chooses to portray a more streamlined appearance.

Ice treats date to the time of the Roman emperor Nero. Each summer he sent slaves into the mountains for snow, which was then flavored with fruit and honey. Ice-making machines were invented in the nineteenth century, and soon the snowball was popular, especially during the hot and humid summers of Baltimore. By the time of the Great Depression, Baltimore led the nation in the consumption of snowballs, also known as "hard times sundaes."

In 1934, Dave Davison, owner of the Davison Candy Company, began using the newly invented electric ice shaver for his snowballs. When he saw how well the machine worked, he acquired the patent from the inventor and, after making several improvements, founded the Sno-Master Manufacturing Company. Many of the 300 to 500 machines produced annually were sold in Baltimore, but each year about a dozen machines were also shipped to Australia, making the Baltimore snowball an export commodity.

THREE

Route 1:
Washington Boulevard

Before being named Washington Boulevard in 1921 and becoming part of the National Highway 1, this major roadway was known by various other names. Following a Susquehannock Indian path, it was reportedly George Washington's route of choice from Virginia to Baltimore on some two dozen occasions, including the trip to his inaugural ceremonies in New York. In 1873, it was called Columbia Street from Paca to Cross Streets, and it was known as Washington Avenue from Cross Street to the tollgate at Kent Street near the Gwynns Falls, where Interstate 95 now crosses the boulevard by the Carroll Park Municipal Golf Course. It has also been known as the Alexandria Road, the Post Road, and the Great Eastern Highway. Some accounts say the road was finally named *Washington Boulevard* to give out-of-town visitors unfamiliar with the area one long roadway to Washington.

Before the influx of heavy automotive traffic, German residents who relocated to the area as large farms were being subdivided referred to the district to the east, around Cross and Warner Streets (the site of the new football stadium), as

Kuh Viertel, or cow quarters, because the roads were muddy and numerous cow trails marked the area. Another area southwest of Washington Boulevard and Cross Street was named *Pigtown*, a name it still retains. Today's Washington Boulevard is noted for its abundance of eating places, motels, gas stations, and other related businesses.

Beneath this sleek, yellow, streamlined exterior lies the heart of a traditional boxy black steam engine, the sole survivor of an effort to refit the five original 4-6-2 Pacific locomotives and turn them into stronger 4-6-4 Hudson type engines. Engine 490, which was built in 1926 by the American Locomotive Works in Richmond, Virginia, now rests in the display yard of the B & O Railroad Museum, founded in 1953 as the world's first museum of railroading and located a few blocks north of the upper end of Washington Boulevard.

When C & O introduced the Sportsman in 1930 as its premier train, Engine 490 served the route until the George Washington took over in 1932. The engine then saw service between Cincinnati, Ohio, and Washington, D.C., until 1942, when the longer and heavier George Washington required stronger pulling power. Engine 490 saw continuous service during World War II, heading up troop trains bound for embarkation points at Newport News, Virginia.

Following the war, the chairman of C & O began an ambitious expansion of passenger operations. He first ordered streamlined cars from the Budd Company and new Baldwin 4-8-0-4-6-4 engines to serve the new Chessie lines. To that end, and at a savings of $85,000 per engine, the war-weary F-19s were rebuilt into super Class L-1 Hudson 4-6-4 engines. In May 1946, Engine 490 entered the Huntington, West Virginia, shop and was stripped down to its empty boiler shell. An extended smokebox and new firebox were added to the rebuilt boiler. Following numerous other modifications and additions, an orange streamlined shroud with fluted stainless steel skirting that matched the new passenger cars was placed over the boiler. These rebuilt engines would prove to be the only streamlined steam locomotives ever owned by the C & O Railroad.

Unfortunately, airline expansion and increased auto production overwhelmed these grandiose plans, and the Chessie passenger trains never ran. Engine 490 was painted yellow in 1950 and was retired from service after her April 1952 daytime trip from Newport News to Charlottesville. She spent the years 1955–71 as part of the locomotive collection in the Historic Huntington Roundhouse and, on April 17, 1971, was moved to the Western Hemisphere's oldest and most significant collection of rail stock and related historical items.

People have been stopping at this unique restaurant since the earliest days of Route 1. The Williams family started the business in 1924 and installed these unusual stools made of plumbing pipes at the outside counter. Over the intervening years and through various owners, the look has remained the same. Since the 1970s, Daniel's Restaurant has been operated by a mother, son, and grandson, and it continues to serve a full menu, whether visitors choose to dine inside or out. Motorcycle enthusiasts of all ages often stop for a meal, especially on a quiet Sunday morning, and the Kiwanis Club holds its regular meetings here.

The prospects for seeing an elk on Washington Boulevard are slim at best, but this sign has been directing weary travelers to a room for the night for many years. With the growth in prosperity and the burgeoning number of cars during the years following World War II, many signs such as this began appearing along the nation's highways. In those days before the interstate system, increasing numbers of local motels gave travelers the advantage of being able to head out on the open road without having to make advance reservations, which allowed them more flexibility in their travel plans. Large chains may have taken away much of the business that these local places used to enjoy, but Route 1 still offers enough traffic to support a few of these one-of-a-kind motels.

FOUR

Wilkens Avenue

Wilkens Avenue owes its establishment to William Wilkens, a German-born immigrant who arrived in the United States with only eighteen cents in his pocket but with plans for making a fortune. Noting that false curls, rats, and chignons were very popular, he decided to manufacture these hairpieces. To earn his capital, he worked as a trader between New Orleans and Texas. He moved to Baltimore in 1843 after deciding it was the best place for his factory. Initially he rented part of Colson's glue factory, then he leased a 100-foot lot on Frederick Road near the Carroll estate in an area known as Snake Hollow. In time, his factory expanded to 15 acres with another 150 acres for his workers' homes. Eventually he employed 700 workers and had branches in New York, Chicago, and St. Louis.

The first telephone service in Baltimore was set up between Wilkens' factory and the Pratt Street warehouse. In addition, Wilkens founded the railroad between Baltimore and Catonsville to the west. Having become one of the city's leading industrialists, he gave more than thirty-three acres to establish Wilkens Avenue as well as the beds of McHenry,

Monroe, and Bentalou Streets. He planted rows of maple and poplar trees and saw to the development of a park along the original seven blocks.

Over the years, the city has twice tried to change the road's name. In 1932 someone suggested Sunset Boulevard, but that was quickly defeated. Then, in 1941, the City Council changed the name to Crozier Boulevard, in honor of a former engineer for Baltimore, but the residents rose up in defense of their road, and the city fathers promptly returned its original name.

Today, Wilkens Avenue, which runs southwest from Gilmore Street to Rolling Road in Catonsville, is noted for having the city's longest unbroken block of yellow brick rowhouses complete with their white marble steps. Developed by Walter L. Westphal, they were built by the B. J. McCullough Company, whose identification as a builder was the ornate balls atop the cornice work.

For almost eighty-five years, this fire department "castle" was the home base for Baltimore City Fire Department's Engine Company 38. Although the company was organized in August 1910, Captain John B. Bortell and his men did not occupy their new quarters until December 10, 1910. From the crenelated roof line to the Gothic arches to the gated entry, the architecture of the two-story stone and brick structure is a holdover from Victorian times, when many buildings resembled castles. Located at West Baltimore Street near Fremont and built for a modest $24,000, it serves as an architectural landmark for the neighborhood. The building remained an active firehouse until September 21, 1994, when the engine company went out of service and the building was sold to private owners.

Residents around the Hollins Market just north of the upper end of Wilkens Avenue may often experience the sensation of being watched, a suspicion that would prove correct if they were to walk by this particular building. In its large front window resides a giant, disgruntled-looking papier-mâché gorilla head, staring out at all who use this route. He was created in the mid-1990s by a local artist as a display for the Sowebo Festival. When the festival ended, the artist decided to leave him on permanent display before a background of giant dice.

Owners of well-coiffed canines in the Arbutus area south of Wilkens Avenue are likely to recognize this storefront, with its orderly gray Formstone, freshly laundered white curtains, and an awning fit for a hotel. Since the poodle popularity of the late 1950s, the Arbutus Poodle Salon has also welcomed terriers, cocker spaniels, and "the all-American house pet" to come in for a bath and a trim.

FIVE

Route 40 West: The Baltimore National Pike

Route 40, stretching from Manhattan Island to Los Angeles, is one of the nation's most historic roads. Following the Louisiana Purchase, Thomas Jefferson realized that there was no connection between the east and the rich lands of the west, so in 1806 he authorized the construction of a road from Cumberland to the headwaters of the navigable Ohio River (now Wheeling, West Virginia). Known as the National Pike, this was the first federal road built in the United States. Baltimore quickly saw the advantage of building a link with Cumberland and this gateway to the west.

Private companies were organized to build these new roads, which were financed with toll fees, and by 1808, the Baltimore and Frederick Town Turnpike Company had completed twenty miles leading out of the city, with another seventeen under construction. The road was known for years as the Frederick Pike because it was an extension of Frederick Avenue. The route out of the city was later switched to Edmondson Avenue when the dual highway was built.

To finance and construct the road from Boonsboro west, the banks were called upon to finance it or lose their charters. By 1820, the "Bank Road" reached Cumberland, leaving a fifteen-mile stretch to be completed. The Hagerstown and Conococheague Turnpike Company built the toll road to the west side of the river, and the banks were approached again under a new threat to their charters to finance the ten-mile gap between Hagerstown and Boonsboro. Completed in 1824, this final section was the first macadam road in America.

The heaviest traffic ever handled by an American road to that time poured the wealth of the west into Baltimore, and a traveler could find taverns every two miles. The opening of the C & O Canal, however, almost drove the turnpike out of business. After the Erie Canal was opened, Baltimore entered one of the most trying times in its commercial history. In 1828, in order to counteract this competition, the city's merchants and businessmen started the Baltimore & Ohio Railroad, the country's first. The laying of the B & O tracks in 1852 through the Allegheny Mountains sounded the death knell for the C & O Canal, and ended the flow of freight traffic on the National Pike.

In 1908, the newly formed State Roads Commission took on the responsibility of building and maintaining a network of major highways. That, combined with the improvement of vehicles after World War I, led to a revival of U.S. Route 40. Today, much of Route 40 west of Baltimore has been absorbed by Interstate Highway 70.

For the past seven or eight years, these giant jolly jokers have cast their grins on the traffic along North Howard

Street. These smiling clown heads are the streetside ambassadors of A. T. Jones & Sons, Inc., costumers to Maryland since 1868.

For many years this company, which claims to be America's oldest in the business, was the only source of formal wear in the city. Following the 1904 fire that destroyed much of downtown Baltimore, the company moved to its present location, where it continues to provide costumes for operatic and theatrical productions, magic shows, and school, church, and lodge shows. It also outfits wax

museums worldwide and provides mascots—most notably the Oriole bird. Not to forget the ultimate in costume-oriented holidays, Halloween brings many private customers through the doors of the shop to request unforgettable costumes for the eerie evening's festivities.

Every day hundreds of drivers roll past this dry-cleaning shop on a busy Route 40 corner in Catonsville, west of the city. From the metal awnings to the numerous signs indicating services available, the message here is all business. After dark, the dramatic flashing arrows no doubt direct customers even more emphatically to the entrance doors.

SIX

Reisterstown Road

Reisterstown Road began as a privately funded turnpike that was used by farmers from as far north as Pennsylvania to transport their livestock and produce to the Baltimore markets. In the early days of the nineteenth century, many turnpikes were maintained by private companies because the state could not afford to finance all the roads it needed. To assure these companies of sufficient revenues, an elaborate system of tolls was established, generally based on a distance of ten miles and further defined by the type and amount of traffic involved. A man on horseback might pay ten cents, while a score of sheep would cost twenty cents. The only vehicles that escaped such regulated payment at the various tollgates were trolleys, because the companies that operated the cars paid a flat fee to the turnpike company.

Tollgates were erected in three places along Reisterstown Road. The first was at Park Circle on the western edge of what is now Druid Hill Park, the second was at Seven Mile Lane in Pikesville, and the third, a double tollgate, was in Owings Mills. The road was actually barred by two heavy gates, which swung back and forth on swivels, pre- venting travel until the appropriate toll was paid. Tolls were collected at the Park Circle gate until 1911, even though the gate and its land had been absorbed by the city's growth to the north. Protests by the Anti-Tollgate League led to the city's purchase of the gate and its land, and the collecting of tolls ceased there.

Located in Druid Hill Park near the southern end of Reisterstown Road in West Baltimore, the Latrobe Pavilion was built in 1864. Known originally as Orem's Way, the ornamented, open building served as a station stop near the Council Grove Pavilion for a small railway that once traveled through the grounds. As late as 1887,

the major means of transportation were horses and carriages and horse-drawn streetcars. Because the streetcar did not run beyond North Avenue, the city's northern boundary, the Park Commission operated a dummy steam engine from the end of the streetcar line to the lake.

This pavilion is one of many park buildings designed by architect George A. Frederick. Born in 1841 in Baltimore to German Catholic parents, Frederick attended local parochial schools then entered the offices of Lind & Murdoch, one of Baltimore's leading architectural firms at the time. He also served for a time with the equally well known firm of Niernsee & Neilson.

At the tender age of twenty-one, Frederick won the competition to design a new City Hall. He reportedly received $10,000 as a down payment, and $10 a day for each day of supervision. The outbreak of the Civil War delayed the building's completion until 1875; when finished, however, it was considered one of the finest and most ambitious municipal structures in the United States and, to Frederick's credit, came in under budget.

Frederick's reputation led to other major jobs, including the buildings for Druid Hill, Patterson, and other public parks. Frederick also designed the house and stable at Cylburn for Jesse Tyson, whose family operated chrome and copper mines in Bare Hills, and the neighboring Rustcombe Mansion for Jesse's brother. Other projects included the 1875 building for City College, a number of private residences, and some Catholic churches. Frederick was also responsible for the renovations to the State Capitol in Annapolis in 1880.

Druid Hill Park, first envisioned by John H. Latrobe, was dedicated on October 19, 1860, and was affectionately called the city's "front yard" because it was the place where everyone could go and enjoy a day in the country. Indeed, when it opened, they poured in from everywhere. In time there was a lake for boating and ice skating, complete with the "Island Lodge," which provided shelter and refreshment for skaters, a zoo, a rose garden, a conservatory, a bandstand, and 675 acres filled with winding paths and roads. During the Civil War, the park was even used for drilling and parading soldiers.

Today's Druid Hill Park continues to be a "front yard" for the citizens of Baltimore, providing them with a source of outdoor recreation in today's busy urban setting.

Captured at the peak of spring, this townhouse on Auchentoroly Terrace demonstrates the careful attention to decorative detail of an earlier era, when Druid Hill Park (which the townhouse faces) was first established. Auchentoroly was the name of the estate before it became a city park.

Originally, the majority of the land was a grant by Charles Calvert, Lord Baltimore, to a Thomas Durbing, who named it "Hab Nab at a Venture," which roughly means "hit or miss." In 1716, Nicholas Rogers II assumed ownership, and the land passed to his daughter, Eleanor. Miss Rogers married a Scottish physician, George Buchanan, who is usually regarded as one of the founders of Baltimore, and he named the estate "Auchentorlie," after his family holdings in Dumbartonshire, Scotland. According to *Johnston's Place Names of Scotland*, *Auchen* is defined as a field or "plough of land," and *Auchentorlie* as a "Field of Sorlie."

Buchanan's granddaughter married Nicholas Rogers, a descendant of the original Rogers, and he renamed the estate "Druid Hill" after the original mansion burned and was rebuilt in 1796. His son, Lloyd, sold the acreage for the park to the city but took little pleasure in the act; his decision to sell was prompted by

near Northern Parkway is the chef from the restaurant's earlier life as a Burger Chef drive-in restaurant, in the days when hamburgers cost fifteen cents apiece. Today, this carry-out restaurant offers a delicious array of ribs, fish, chicken, homemade dinner rolls, and many different vegetables.

Pikesville

Reisterstown Road travels through the heart of Pikesville, a community that was established in 1770, when the Beacham house was built. More homes followed, and Pikesville became a convenient overnight stop for wagons and stagecoaches traveling between Baltimore and York, Pennsylvania. In 1794, the Old Burnt Tavern served as an inn for travelers and as a gathering place where townsmen from Baltimore Towne, the community of Soldiers' Delight Hundred, and the county seat of Joppa could learn the news of the day.

Pikesville takes its name from a hero of the War of 1812, General Zebulon Pike, for whom Pike's Peak in Colorado was also named. In 1814 Dr. James Smith, the first American doctor to immunize patients for smallpox, purchased a tract of land along the highway leading north from Baltimore. Two years later, he sold a fourteen-acre tract to the U.S. government for use as an arsenal. This site was selected because it was considered to be at a safe distance from Baltimore in case it blew up. Later, the military post became the Maryland Line Confederate Soldiers' Home. It now serves as State Police barracks and a community area.

his feeling of resentment over the city's effort to condemn a portion of his land for a turnpike. A political mess nearly prevented the conclusion of the sale, but it finally went through, with the purchase being financed by the one-cent railway tax.

Lurking beneath the dramatic red paint of this sign on Reisterstown Road

Poised like rockets to the moon, these ice cream cones have been part of the Pikesville skyline since the early 1960s. They are part of a patented design developed in the 1930s by company founder Tom Carvel, who later gave the design to McDonald's.

When Carvel was four, his family emigrated from Greece and settled in New York City. In his teens and early twenties, he held many different jobs in the city, but ill health forced him to move to the country. In an effort to make some money, he borrowed fifteen dollars from his girlfriend (who later became his wife) and bought a truckload of ice cream. When the truck broke down in Hartsdale, New York, he had to sell the ice cream on the spot. Because it sold well and he liked the area, he decided to stay there. He founded the Carvel Company in 1934.

During the early years, Carvel concentrated on developing the equipment and the product line; later his company became the first in the United States to franchise locations. In 1954, Tom Carvel won the Horatio Alger award, and he went on to hold more than two hundred patents and trademarks for his work. When he retired in 1989, he sold the company to Investcorp International. Today there are four hundred fifty retail outlets on the East Coast, of which only a hundred retain this early design.

The art deco facade of the Pikes Theater, which opened its doors in 1937, was designed by Baltimore native John F. Eyring (1897–1963). After attending the Maryland Institute, College of Art, the U.S. Coast Guard Academy, and the School of Architecture of the University of Pennsylvania, he opened his own architectural firm in 1927. Besides the Pikes, he also designed the Strand, Vilma, Uptown, and Carlton theaters. His father's company, E. Eyring & Sons, built the Pikes and several of Baltimore's other grand movie houses.

For many years, the Pikes was run by the Beck Organization as a neighborhood theater. Then, in the spring of 1968, JF Theaters leased the Pikes, which soon became a first-run house. Patrons got more than they bargained for on March 1, 1968, when everyone had to be evacuated during a screening of *The Graduate* after an oil burner exploded. The blast blew the outside furnace room doors some fifteen feet into the parking lot and moved a section of the rear wall an inch outward.

After fifty years of service, the Pikes finally closed its doors. Various efforts to develop the building into a cultural arts center have met with little success. Plans for converting it into an Italian gourmet food center are being pursued, but at present it remains a vacant reminder of a time when movie houses were grand.

SEVEN

Falls Road

In the eighteenth century Falls Road was, like many other roads in Maryland, an Indian trail. When the General Assembly passed the enabling legislation in 1804, the Falls Road Turnpike Company was incorporated, and plans were devised to run a road from the crossroads near Richard Caton's lime kiln in Baltimore County south to the city, hugging the line of the Jones Falls. This early five-mile segment stretched from Brooklandville to Baltimore. Further construction was undertaken in 1807 to unite the trade of the north with Baltimore and provide a direct line to Hanover and Carlisle, in Pennsylvania. Many feeder roads extended beyond Carlisle, enabling wagons laden with produce to travel down the turnpike from the north and west and return carrying salt and groceries. Many quarries were located along Falls Road, as well as mills that used the water from the Jones Falls to provide power for the manufacture of such items as cotton duck for Baltimore's clipper ships.

Most of today's heavy traffic is carried by Interstate 83 to the east, but a traveler can still follow Falls Road from its origin in the city just south of the Streetcar Museum.

Along the route north one can see mill buildings adapted to new uses, old established neighborhoods, newly constructed suburbs, family farms, and horse pastures as the road passes through communities such as Hampden, Mount Washington, Bare Hills, and Butler on its way to where it ends near the Pennsylvania line.

A visitor to Baltimore coming off the Jones Falls Expressway to cross the Twenty-eighth Street bridge near the southern end of Falls Road might cast a wary glance at these giant reptiles as they march across the bridge. This trio of huge but harmless beasts represents the work of Baltimore artist John Ellsberry, who painted them in 1986 as one of ten murals in the city's revamped mural program. The early years of the current program were actually part of an antigraffiti effort sponsored through the Mayor's Advisory Committee on Art and Culture by the Coordinating Committee on Criminal Justice. For the most part, graffiti artists rarely leave their marks on these creations, recognizing perhaps the enormous effort, skill, and inspiration necessary to produce such large-scale paintings.

Ellsberry began his design with a single beast but quickly decided to add two more because they worked so well with the shape of the wall. While he and two assistants were hard at work, many motorists stopped and offered words of gratitude and encouragement. Other residents expressed initial concern over his choice of subject matter, feeling it to be predatory in nature, but they voiced their appreciation soon after the mural's completion. This appreciation has continued through the years, as more and more residents take note of the charming mural. Ellsberry recalls giving a neighbor a ride that took them past the bridge art. Unaware of Ellsberry's connection, the neighbor told him that each day when he picked up his daughter from school, she asked to be driven past the alligators. When Ellsberry told him he had painted them, the neighbor was surprised to discover he knew the person who had actually created the locally renowned work that brought his daughter so much pleasure.

Since first appearing, the alligator mural has twice been voted "Best Mural in Baltimore" by the *City Paper*'s annual poll. In addition to these marching monsters, Ellsberry has painted a mural of Billie Holiday downtown and two train murals across from the B & O Railroad Museum. Besides painting murals, Ellsberry works as a photographer and creates stained glass tile mosaics.

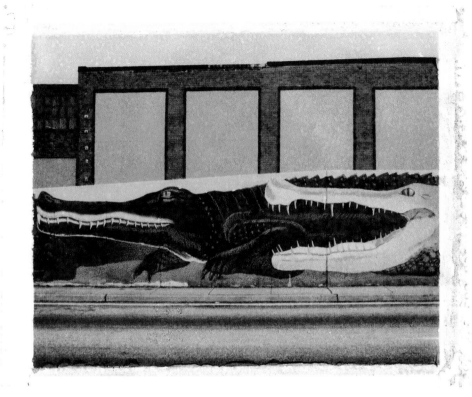

Every day, work-weary commuters stream past this modest seafood shop on Twenty-ninth Street on their way to the nearby Jones Falls Expressway, which parallels the lower section of Falls Road. And for more than fifty years, passersby have stopped to purchase their favorite seafood, especially crab cakes, haddock, and shrimp. The owners of Sterling's are now serving their fourth generation of customers, many of whom drive long distances from the counties in order to take home their favorite carryout seafood.

Hampden

The mill community of Hampden, which lies along Falls Road just south of Roland Park, dates to the early 1800s, when cotton duck mills began operation, using the waters of the Jones Falls to power their machinery. The cotton duck produced at these mills was used to make the sails for Baltimore's early clipper ships. Other businesses in the area included grist mills and iron foundries. The name of this community was given by landowner Henry Mankin in honor of John Hampden, a seventeenth-century statesman whom he admired.

In today's Hampden, many of the old mill buildings have been converted to artists' studios and offices for a wide variety of businesses. The community is enjoying the attention of people from all over the city, as well as an influx of new shops, restaurants, and other establishments.

Faded from years of exposure, this painted sign for the Hampden Transfer and Storage Company on Falls Road cleverly shows a roadside billboard painted in perspective against a landscaped background. Company manager Edwin Parrish had it painted in 1951 in response to a convention talk he heard on the value of outdoor advertising. Because Parrish already had a large clock and sign in front of his office, he decided people might be doubly impressed with his company's name if he used the wall behind the clock as well. He then turned the job over to the Belsinger Sign Works, and they created this sign within a sign.

The Hampden Transfer and Storage Company was founded by B. H. Barnes in 1895, when horse and wagon was the mode of travel. Edwin Parrish purchased it five years later and remained active in the business until 1960. The family's original home, which was part of the business, continues to serve as the company's offices. One of the early trucks could be converted to an open-air tour bus by rolling up its canvas sides and putting thirty-four chairs in the cargo area, thereby generating extra income for the company. When Parrish decided to retire, he sold the moving company to the Von Paris family, who chose to leave the company's well-known name in place. The rug cleaning business was purchased by the Sunderland family, who renamed it the Chesapeake-Hampden Rug and Drapery Cleaners.

This sign will be hidden from view when the owner of the building on which it appears paints his own sign, and another link to the past will be lost.

Located on the southern edge of Roland Park to the east of Falls Road, these charming Victorian cottages have been prominent landmarks since they were built in 1861 by architect Edward MacDonald Greenway Jr. He built the largest of the three houses for himself, his wife, and young children and the two smaller cottages for his married daughters. Early in their construction, Greenway discovered that he had no money to build the stairs in his own four-level home, so the project became known as "Greenway's Follies." Between them, the three homes also contain other oddities, including an underground passage that led to a now demolished stone stable on the north side, windows of different sizes in the same room, a fireplace in a closet, and a very high door in the darkest part of the second floor, which opens into a steep, narrow stairway.

From 1916 to 1980, Roland Park Country School, a private girls' school, occupied the properties, and the houses were used as residences for the faculty. One visitor during those years claimed to have seen a ghost in the largest house. Residents of Roland Park Place, a retirement community, now occupy the homes.

Mount Washington

Mount Washington came into being as a fashionable suburb of Baltimore in the middle of the nineteenth century, when George Gelbach Jr. purchased part of a tract of land called Edward's and Will's Hills and Valleys and began promoting it as a rural retreat from the city, but the community's roots go back to an earlier time.

The Washington Cotton Manufacturing Company established Maryland's first cotton mill in 1819. With the development of a copper mine in nearby Bare Hills, the small mill village of Washingtonville soon appeared. Twenty years later, the Baltimore and Susquehanna Railroad laid track through the Jones Valley. Then, in 1855, the German Reformed Church opened the Mount Washington Female Academy, a finishing school for young ladies of the North and the South. The Civil War forced its closing in 1861, and, despite the efforts of other schools, it remained closed until 1867, when Charles Dougherty purchased the property for the Sisters of Mercy's new Mount Saint Agnes Academy, named in honor of his wife. Initially an elementary-secondary school, it became a college in 1890, but money problems continually plagued the academy, forcing it to close and reopen parts of the school several times. Finally, in 1971, it merged with Loyola College in Baltimore and leased its property in Mount Washington. In 1979 a local developer purchased the campus, hoping to build a planned community. In 1982, the property was purchased by the USF&G Company as part of its expansion.

No longer a suburb of Baltimore, Mount Washington continues to be a desirable community, one whose mill areas along Falls Road are enjoying new life as they are redeveloped for present-day use.

Each of the happy faces on this mural belongs to one of the students who helped to paint it in the late 1980s. This colorful composition represents the creative collaboration of students, parents, and teachers at the Mount Wash-ington Elementary School, located on Sulgrave Avenue west of Falls Road. While parents and teachers drew and painted the larger elements of the mural, each of the 330 children was encouraged to paint his or her own face. The students were then asked to add a selection of their favorite activities—which turned out to be baseball for some and dreams of flying in hot air balloons for others.

Tucked in a tiny front garden on Lake Avenue near Falls Road in Mount Washington is this finely crafted topiary delight. When Maria and Allan Taylor bought the 150-year-old house in 1976, it had nothing but a plain front lawn and a small privet hedge, so they decided to do something more interesting. At first, Mrs. Taylor sculpted bears for herself and ducks for her husband. Then people began making suggestions, and she added a cat, a dog, a fox, an alligator, and even a well-endowed tree. Someone even wanted a turkey, but that proved too difficult to sculpt out of leaves.

Completely self-taught, Mrs. Taylor uses only pruning shears and handclippers to sculpt the privet, yew, cedar, spruce, and boxwood that surround the house. She sees a subject in an overgrown shrub in the way that Michelangelo saw a form in a piece of marble. Her job is to snip away what is unnecessary, and that job is pure pleasure.

Topiary art dates from the first century A.D., when a friend of the Roman emperor Augustus began to train shrubs and border hedges. Later, it became fashionable to sculpt hedges into cones, spires, and columns as garden accents. Whimsy soon took over, especially in England, and leafy horses could be found "jumping" over hedges, following equally leafy hounds.

Farther north on Falls Road, the hand-painted sign of this independent rug cleaner urges its customers to do some of the work and save themselves some money. Founded in 1947 by Paul Spangler and his two partners, the original location on Old York Road near Memorial Stadium proved to be too small. After venturing out Falls Road to the country, the owner selected this Bare Hills site, where the shop has expanded three times. According to the founder's son, Wayne, who was a small boy at the time, there was not much beyond a gas station and a house in the area when the shop relocated there.

After several years Mr. Spangler bought out his partners, and the family-run business, now in its third generation, has customers who bring their carpets from as far away as Maine, New Jersey, and Virginia. Regulars have included Rosa Ponselle, members of the Baltimore Colts and the Orioles, and various television and radio personalities. Longtime customers know not to "lug their rugs" during the noon hour, though, because the owners sensibly close the doors for lunch.

In preparation for the shop's fiftieth anniversary, the very first invoice written in April 1947 was discovered, indicating that a nine-by-twelve rug pad was dustcleaned for the sum of $2.16—including pickup and delivery.

EIGHT

Charles Street

Maryland Route 139, better known as Charles Street, is one of the oldest thoroughfares in the United States, and it began when Baltimore began—that is, when the General Assembly passed an act in 1731 "for erecting a towne on the North side of the Patapsco, and for laying out lots, in and about the place where one John Fleming now lives." Mr. Fleming lived in a tenant house on the property of David and Charles Carroll near the spot where the USF&G building stands today, just south of Lombard Street. Charles Street now stretches from Winder Street in South Baltimore north to Interstate 695—the Beltway—and serves as the east-west divider for the city. (Baltimore Street is the north-south divider.)

Several theories have been offered as to how Charles Street received its name. Many think it is a tribute to Charles Carroll of Carrollton. Others believe that the name refers to "Charles, one of the Lords of Baltimore," a theory that has merit, since Baltimore was founded "in the 15th year of the Dominion of the Right Honourable Charles, Absolute Lord and Propietary of the Province of Maryland and Avalon."

Earlier names included Forest, or Forrest, Street and one stretch was known as Goodman Street.

The earliest known paving of Charles Street was done with cobblestones in 1799, which were followed by a succession of wooden blocks, asphalt blocks, Belgian blocks, and granite blocks before the use of sheet asphalt.

Among the many important events that have occurred along its length is the lighting of the first Christmas tree in Baltimore by a German merchant named Bredermeyer, whose house near North Avenue later became the headquarters of the Union Club during the Civil War. There was also a famous dueling ground in a grove on the site of the old Stafford Hotel (now apartments) in Mount Vernon.

High above the traffic that travels daily on the section of Charles Street known as Washington Place is this reminder of the smallest of the city's better hotels of the past. Dr. William A. Moale built the Stafford on the site of his father's house in 1894. Designed as an apartment house, it was operated as a hotel with many family suites, where some residents reportedly lived for decades. Located at the heart of the fashionable district in Baltimore, it was the site of many social events in the years before the opening of the Belvedere three blocks to the north, and it welcomed many famous people of the time—including F. Scott Fitzgerald, who lived there for several months.

In the 1960s, theatrical troupes, musical groups, and students from the nearby Peabody Conservatory of Music

occupied many of its rooms. English tailors and bootmakers, in particular, chose to stay at the Stafford whenever they were in town. With the decline of the hotel business, the Stafford Hotel was sold at auction in the mid-1970s, and it has served as an apartment building ever since.

On December 14, 1903, where Chase Street meets Charles, the beautiful Belvedere Hotel celebrated its grand opening. Designed in the Beaux-Arts style by local architects Douglas H. Thomas Jr. and J. Hatleston Parker, the hotel wasted no time in becoming a major presence in the social life of Baltimore. People were often heard telling their friends, "Meet me at the Belvedere."

The Belvedere's prime location had once been a part of Howard's Woods and the site of one of John Eager Howard's homes, for which it was named. Built at a cost of $1,750,000, it boasted many luxuries, and the management proudly claimed that it was the first hotel in Baltimore to have all its windows completely fly-screened.

Though recent years have seen the hotel rooms converted to condominiums, the sumptuous Owl Bar still provides a favorite meeting place for those seeking food and drink. And the Belvedere often serves as a backdrop for many occasions, both real and fictitious, such as a wedding celebration in Barry Levinson's *Homicide: Life on the Streets*, the NBC police drama series set in Baltimore.

A sense of mystery surrounds this sign in a window above East Preston Street near Charles. It actually marks the site of a club that was formed in 1921 for the benefit of hearing impaired people who are interested in participatory sports. Now the oldest club of its kind in the United States, the Silent Oriole Club owes its existence to a city policeman who once told a group of deaf men that they had to do something besides stand on the street all day. With his help, they found a place to meet and began the organization, which has grown to one hundred fifty members. Because the participants cannot hear, the clubhouse has such helpful features as a flashing light instead of a doorbell, and the club shows captioned films for its viewing audience. It provides sports and social activities as well as vocational help to its members and is part of a nationwide chain of clubs that belongs to the Amateur Athletic Association of the Deaf.

This decorative triptych located above the Schuler School's first floor windows, as well as other outside decorations, were designed by noted Baltimore sculptor Hans Schuler. The building, which served as his studio, is located east of Charles Street and was designed by Baltimore architect William Gordon Beecher, as was the family home next door. When built in 1906, the studio was unique on the East Coast because it had twenty-two-foot-high ceilings and a crane with which to move Schuler's massive sculptures.

Born in the Lorraine province of Germany in 1874, Schuler was six years old when his parents brought him to Baltimore. When he was graduated from the Maryland Institute for the Promotion of the Mechanical Arts at age twenty, he won three medals and a scholarship from the Charcoal Club which allowed him to attend the Rinehart School of Sculpture. After graduation, a scholarship from the Rinehart School allowed him to study at the Julian Academy in Paris. There he sculpted *Ariadne*, one of his best known pieces, which won him a gold medal from the Paris Salon. He was only the fifth American to win the award at that time. When he returned to America, he designed and sculpted works of art that are on public view all over the city, including the bust of Johns Hopkins in front of the University's Homewood campus and the memorial to General Sam Smith in Wyman Park.

Schuler also served as an instructor and later as the director of the renamed Maryland Institute of Fine and Practical Art, and he became embroiled in a debate over the clash between traditional and modernist art before his death, in 1951. Eight years later, the Schuler School was formed when his son, Hans C. Schuler Jr., and his daughter-in-law, Anne Didusch Schuler, left the Maryland Institute in order to teach art students in the traditional ways of the old masters in an atelier, or studio, setting.

In addition to Schuler's studio and home, architect William Gordon Beecher designed many buildings in Baltimore, including the Emerson Hotel and its additions, the Electrical Engineering and Civil Engineering buildings at the Johns Hopkins University's Homewood campus, a number of private homes, and several churches (among them the Catonsville Presbyterian Church, which he attended). He and Hans Schuler collaborated on the Buchanan Memorial in Washington, D.C., for the National Commission of Fine Arts. In the early 1930s, Beecher worked to beautify Washington and Mount Vernon Places with magnolias, azaleas, and Japanese cherry trees. From 1934 to 1946, when Beecher was chief architect for the Baltimore office of the Federal Housing Administration, he designed the Venti-Lite Home, a group dwelling he felt would challenge the conventional rowhouse and surpass the average detached home in livability, light, air, view, and privacy.

On the southeast corner of the intersection of Charles Street and North Avenue, many a pedestrian has walked beneath this expressive character without ever being aware of his presence, hovering above the second story, gazing down on the activities below. Gargoyles, of which there are many fine examples in Baltimore, were first developed in Milan, Italy, and were originally used to ornament waterspouts. Later they were developed into decorative features, as represented by this amusing example.

The first general meeting of the company to be held outside Atlanta took place in Baltimore in 1923 at the Southern Hotel. All the top officers were in attendance to mark the opening of what was then the world's largest soft drink factory—which could produce 3.5 million cases (70 million bottles) a year, an enormous amount at that time. Baltimore had one of the largest of the eight syrup manufacturing plants in the country. Syrup was shipped in jugs, kegs, barrels, and stainless steel drums to one hundred thousand soda fountains and eleven hundred bottlers.

In 1935, the Atlanta home office chose Baltimore as the site for its Research Department, which would have full charge of the chemical formulas and flavoring for all the products. Then, in 1941, the Kirk Avenue plant, which had been completed in the spring of 1939, was awarded a certificate of merit by the Baltimore Association of Commerce, recognizing it as being the best in design and construction of all the buildings erected in 1939 in the city. That same year also saw the beginning of construction for a branch plant at Ostend and Hamburg Streets.

Baltimore's Coca-Cola company was one of ten still owned by the parent company in 1980, but those ties came to an end when it was sold to the Mid-Atlantic Coca-Cola Bottling Company in that same year.

Charles Village

Charles Village was known as Peabody Heights in 1870, when five area businessmen formed a company of the same name in order to create an exclusive, upper-class, upper-income community within the suburbs of Baltimore.

Also high above North Avenue is this fading reminder of a popular soft drink that has early and strong ties to Baltimore. The local branch of the Atlanta, Georgia–based company, founded in 1886, dates from 1905. At that time it had four employees, who produced the first bottle of Coca-Cola in Baltimore in the basement of 665 West Saratoga Street. Later the company moved to the Candler Building on Pratt Street and then, in 1920, to East Fort Avenue in South Baltimore.

At the time, North Avenue to the south was the city line. The five men were a Baptist minister, a soap- and candlemaker, a brick manufacturer, and two real-estate brokers. As part of their grandiose plan, they established stiff building guidelines for their community. There were to be particular size standards; a setback of twenty feet; and no slaughterhouses, offensive manufacturing establishments, beer saloons, or buildings that would increase insurance rates on adjacent properties. However, by 1890 there was no neighborhood, and a large section of the land was sold to Frances Yewell, who built thirty-six homes.

In 1943, when Grace Darin moved to the neighborhood, the area was named University Heights, but over the years people expressed a desire for a different name. Darin chose the name *Charles Village* in 1967 after considering the new Charles Center and the folksy concept of a village within a city. Today, Charles Village is a comfortable collection of attractive Roman brick buildings with an assortment of flat and squared facades crowned by slate roof caps.

When the Charles Village area was being developed, strict covenants were implemented, and among the few businesses allowed in the residential neighborhood were drugstores. Located at Charles and Twenty-fifth Streets since before the turn of the century, this beautiful building, with its distinctive crescent moon roof decoration, was known as Hayes' Pharmacy and then as Codd's Pharmacy. Under either name, the pharmacy was always a favorite place to meet.

When Dr. John Nicholas Codd, a 1907 graduate of the University of Maryland, decided to relocate to Severna Park in the 1930s, he sold his building and business to John B. Thomas Jr. of Thomas & Thompson Pharmaceuticals, a Baltimore firm with retail locations at Baltimore and Light Streets and at Charles and

the 1980s, a sign shop and a drycleaner occupied the location; soon afterward this building and the one next door were purchased by the Copy Cat Printing Company.

Known officially as the Gatehouse, this attractive gray stone building is nestled in a wooded setting next to the Baltimore Museum of Art, near Charles Street. It was built around 1870 as the gardener's cottage, on the main approach from Charles Street to Homewood Villa, the home of William Wyman from 1853 to 1903.

Wyman and his bride received the house as a wedding present from his father, Samuel G. Wyman, who moved from Massachusetts in 1816 and became one of the city's wealthy merchants. Architect Richard Upjohn based his Italian Villa design on the Edward King Villa in Newport, Rhode Island. The elder Wyman named the house Homewood Villa to distinguish it from the original Homewood, which he bought in 1839. Original sketches of Homewood Villa show that the tiny gatehouse was designed with a miniature cupola and ornate triple windows similar to those of the main house.

When William Wyman died in 1903, he left his estate to the Johns Hopkins University but reserved the use of the house to his daughter for her lifetime. Although she never lived in it after her father's death, she maintained the house as it was on the day he died. From 1920 until her death, in 1949, at the age of ninety-two, she lived at the Stafford Hotel but each afternoon took a taxi to Homewood Villa, where she would reminisce about her childhood, returning

Centre Streets. The company was founded in 1872 by Thomas's father, John B. Thomas Sr., and Albert Thompson; the two had met in pharmacy school and gone into business together following graduation. Thomas leased the business to his brother, Oscar, who ran the corner pharmacy. The building also contained four apartments upstairs and a barbershop that was located in the back, next to the alley on Twenty-fifth Street.

In 1978, John B. Thomas III, the grandson of the founder, sold the retail business to Heneson's Pharmacy, the last drugstore to occupy the building. Then, in to her apartment at midnight or later. Upon her death, the house and the remaining money in Wyman's estate went to the University.

During the 1920s and 1930s, the University's engineering department used the little cottage as a laboratory. Then, in 1930, the chemical engineering department assumed control and used it both as a student lab and as housing for students in their program. Since 1965, the carefully maintained building has been home to the offices of the University's newsletter.

Located on Cold Spring Lane a few blocks west of Charles Street, the art deco facade of this restaurant, which is reminiscent of shiny diners and streamlined trains, has been a favorite meeting place for residents and visitors alike for over sixty years.

Founder Isaac "Poppa" Alonso left Spain as a boy to work with his uncle in the Cuban sugarcane fields. Following a move to the United States and a job in a Virginia boatyard, he joined the U.S. Army at the outbreak of World War I and served in France with the 188th Aero Squadron, where he specialized in maintaining the synchronizing mechanisms that allowed machine guns to fire through the aircrafts' propellers. At war's end, he returned to Baltimore, where he met and married his wife, in 1920.

During the 1920s, before deciding to enter the restaurant business, Mr. Alonso had owned a B. F. Goodrich franchise in Cuba, where he sold tire repair kits. When a tropical

storm wiped him out, he and his wife decided to return to Baltimore, where he used his bonus money from his wartime service to open a small eatery on Erdman Avenue near Brehms Lane. From there, he moved west to Roland Park, where he operated "Joe's Place," across the street from his present location.

The decision to move and open Alonso's was aided by an inquiry from a local builder who was putting up houses and who asked Mr. Alonso if he wanted a building for a larger restaurant. Alonso replied that he would, if the builder would put an apartment upstairs, which of course was done. Over the years the eatery became well known for its homemade food (especially pizza and large, juicy hamburgers), and, until his retirement in 1974, Mr. Alonso actively managed the business. Even after he had turned over the reins to his son, he was still very visible, welcoming patrons as they came in to dine. He died in his apartment upstairs on Christmas Eve of 1983, at the age of ninety-one.

NINE

The York Road

Beginning as Greenmount Avenue at its southern end in Baltimore City, the York Road has a long and productive history that dates back to 1741. During that year, in a never-ending effort to expand their trade, Baltimore's merchants and shippers set their sights on the interior north beyond the state's border and established their first liaison with a like-minded group from York, Pennsylvania. That successful meeting marked the beginning of the York Road.

Details about the road's use during its first two years are not known, but in 1743 a representative from Pennsylvania wrote a report indicating the values of this connection, and interstate trade had presumably increased. By late 1751, at least sixty wagons loaded with flaxseed had reportedly traveled down from the north. A few years later, in an effort to maintain the road, Baltimore County appointed sixty-one overseers — indicating the importance of the road to the area's economy.

Until 1787, the county had made every effort to keep the road public, but the county roads were in such poor condition, especially in winter, that the county authorized the building of a series of turnpikes, including one from Baltimore Town toward York, ending at the Baltimore County line. This effort was also unsuccessful, and, in 1804, private turnpike companies were chartered by the General Assembly. One of the first of these companies built the York Road to the Pennsylvania line; it

Though not completed until October 1954, Baltimore's Memorial Stadium, with its classic 1950s modern style, hosted its first football game in September 1953 and its first baseball game in April 1954. The brushed aluminum letters, specially designed for the stadium, were considered by many to be too modern and of an inappropriate character at the time, but fans quickly adopted the stadium as one of their most cherished landmarks.

Ten years of campaigning went into planning and construction, with money issues figuring prominently in each phase of the stadium's history. In June 1947, the Stadium Commission and city officials proposed a joint city and state war memorial, but the governor declared that no state funds were available. At one point, in an effort to save money, then Mayor Thomas D'Alesandro wanted city engineers to draw up the plans themselves, but that proved unworkable. The firm of Faisant and Kooken was awarded the job, and in August 1948 they set up a display of the model in the Stafford Hotel.

Early discussions leaned toward the selection of a different site, but there had been a stadium here since 1922, and so, despite a lawsuit filed by stadium neighbors in December 1947, the present site was maintained. Difficulty over complying with the city's building codes further delayed action. Then the issue of a name erupted, when the Park Board voted to name the stadium after Babe Ruth, even though it had been planned as a war memorial. That prompted action by the Gold Star Mothers, who threatened to use all their energies to defeat the new stadium loan. They contended that if the stadium was a memorial to Maryland's war casualties (from World Wars I and II), it was inappro-

continued to operate for more than a hundred years until, in 1908, the General Assembly formed the State Roads Commission. In 1911, the York Road once again became an open, toll-free road.

Although a traveler can still drive the winding road from Baltimore City to the York area, the vast majority of today's traffic uses the dual-lane Interstate 83 highway, which parallels the York Road from the Baltimore Beltway northward.

priate that it honor Babe Ruth, who had not served in either war. The Gold Star Mothers felt it would be better to honor him with a memorial at St. Mary's Industrial School instead. Yielding to public pressure, the Mayor's Stadium Committee subsequently approved *Baltimore Memorial Stadium* as the official name.

Professional football left the stadium when the National Football League Baltimore Colts moved to Indianapolis in 1984. The Baltimore Orioles played their final baseball game on Thirty-third Street on September 26, 1991, before moving to the newly constructed Oriole Park at Camden Yards. In the 1990s, the short-lived Canadian Football League Stallions used the stadium for their games, as have the NFL Baltimore Ravens, who played their final game there on December 14, 1997, before moving to a new football stadium near Camden Yards. However, nothing can replace the memories of football games past, when screaming fans led sportswriter Cooper Rollow to refer to Memorial Stadium as "the world's largest outdoor insane asylum."

If local movie patrons want to experience the days of Baltimore's grand movie houses, they only have to visit the Senator Theatre on York Road, where current owner Tom Kiefaber, grandson of original owner Frank Durkee, endeavors to maintain its glory. Surprisingly, the Senator was built in only six months' time as just another theater in the Durkee Enterprises chain, which in its heyday operated forty-one theaters, including the Grand, the Patterson, the Boulevard, the Towson, and the Circle in Annapolis. But

the art deco design and attention to quality of architect John J. Zink assured the Senator's success.

Art deco, which was popular in the United States in the 1920s and 1930s, is based on the 1925 Paris Exposition Internationale Modernes, and features streamlined curves, ziggurats, sunbursts, waves, waterfalls, and polychrome effects with combinations of brick, terra cotta, and metal. Zink took the skyscraper style, as seen in the Chrysler Building in New York, and adapted it to movie theaters.

John J. Zink, born in Baltimore in 1886, designed more than thirty movie houses on the East Coast during his career. His early training at the Maryland Institute was followed by work for the firm of Wyatt & Nolting. Prior to World War I, he studied theater architecture under Thomas Lamb in New York and attended the Columbia School of Architecture in the evenings before returning to Baltimore in 1918. Zink, who kept his work plain, was particularly interested in the technical aspects of a building, such as its sight lines and acoustics, features that are both very evident at the Senator. He used many curved surfaces, and he handpicked and steamfitted the matched walnut paneling in the lobby.

When the Senator opened on October 5, 1939, patrons paid twenty cents a ticket to see Spencer Tracy and Sir Cedric Hardwicke in *Stanley and Livingstone*. The program noted that the Senator was "designed along strictly modern lines, constructed of brick with a facade of translucent glass brilliantly illuminated with an array of many colored lights." The curved lobby with its marble floor featured tropical fish in the wall displays, and a "unique sunburst lighting fixture" in the ceiling of the auditorium.

Since purchasing the Senator in 1988, when Durkee Enterprises decided to sell many of its theaters, Tom Kiefaber has worked diligently to maintain it, a formidable task at best. In 1989 the theater was placed on the National Register of Historic Places, and in 1991 a readers' poll by *USA Today* voted it as one of the four best theaters in the United States. Ongoing plans include the restoration of the entire theater to its original condition.

TEN

Loch Raven Boulevard

Although it begins at Greenmount Avenue below Twenty-fifth Street, Loch Raven Boulevard is best known for its beautiful dual-lane section, which begins at the intersection of The Alameda and goes north to Taylor Avenue before joining Interstate 695 just north of Joppa Road. The people who planned the boulevard in the late 1920s hoped that it would someday connect the city with the Loch Raven Reservoir and eventually reach the Prettyboy Dam area. They considered Loch Raven Boulevard more than an ordinary city street or state highway; they saw it as a link with the city's park system because it gave access to the formal entrance of Clifton Park, ran close to Herring Run Park, and touched the Mount Pleasant Golf Course. To them, Loch Raven Boulevard suggested a welcome escape to open woods and hills, pleasant farmlands, and peaceful valleys.

Work began in 1932 and was carried out by Works Progress Administration employees. The southbound lane was completed first, with the northbound lane following in the fall of 1936. Today, the Boulevard's well-planned beauty continues to enhance its appeal as a major north-south route, carrying countless commuters to and from their activities in the city and county.

What hard-core diner enthusiast could resist the glowing neon signs of this eatery, located on Loch Raven Boulevard just south of the Baltimore Beltway? Named for the Beltway and Loch Raven Boulevard, this diner has been serving up its delicious meals since 1964. Open twenty-four hours a day, seven days a week (except Christmas), the Bel-Loc Diner reports that its most popular meal is breakfast, when omelettes top the list of preferred selections. The beautiful building that houses the diner was designed and built by DeRaffle Manufacturing of New Rochelle, New York, and projects that welcoming quality so often found in diners that predate this one.

Residents of the Baynesville community of Baltimore have been stopping at the sign of this happy crab to buy fresh seafood for more than twenty years. Although it now has a seasoned crab-shack appearance, the building was originally a house, before Mo Manocheh, of Mo's Fisherman's Wharf in Little Italy, converted it. Now it is one of many businesses on this busy section of Joppa Road, several blocks east of Loch Raven Boulevard.

ELEVEN

Harford Road

Harford Road was little more than a country lane when it was named in 1770 for Sir Henry Harford. In 1792, General Sam Smith, a veteran of the Revolutionary War, began purchasing large parcels of land on either side of the road between what is now Lake Montebello in Herring Run Park and Woodbourne Avenue to the north as a site for his home, Montebello, in 1820.

State legislation in 1804 saw this thoroughfare developed into the Harford Turnpike, one of the main toll roads out of Baltimore. Maryland turned to these private toll roads out of necessity, because the counties were unable to fund the good roads they knew were essential to furthering the economy of the state.

On its way north from Biddle Street, where it meets Aisquith Street in the city, Harford Road borders Clifton Park, cuts through Herring Run Park, and crosses both the Gunpowder River and the Little Gunpowder Falls before reaching the southern edge of the town of Bel Air, in Harford County.

Today, as Maryland Route 147, Harford Road continues to be a busy and important thoroughfare, passing through well-established communities such as Lauraville, Hamilton, and Parkville before crossing Interstate 695 on its way to Bel Air.

This dramatic mural, located at Harford Road and North Avenue in East Baltimore, demonstrates one of the many ways the city has turned plain blank walls into streetside works of art. In this 1991 painting, titled *However Far the Stream Flows*, Baltimore native Tom Miller wanted to portray the value of exercising the mind by showing an African-American man reading a book. His exotic setting further shows that by reading, a man can be anywhere he chooses or imagines himself to be.

Miller painted this mural, and another directly across the street, in 1996, as part of Baltimore's mural program, which is administered by the Mayor's Advisory Committee on Art and Culture, Department of Housing and Community Development, Business and Assistance Group. Each year, mural sites are chosen around the city and artists are invited to submit designs in competition for the opportunity to execute their compositions. Each selected artist receives a stipend and the materials needed to complete the work.

A well-known area artist, Miller began his career by making brightly colored, boldly designed furniture. In more recent years, he has turned his talents to two-dimensional art, using the same bold colors, geometric shapes, and attitudes that characterize his three-dimensional work. He recently illustrated the children's book, *Can a Coal Scuttle*

Fly?, by Camay Calloway Murphy, and he has produced art for logos, prints, posters, and other mural designs.

Located on Harford Road near North Avenue, the Apollo Theater dates to 1921, when it was one of twelve area theaters constructed during the early years of the golden age of moving pictures (1921–29). Its distinctive facade above the marquee was dominated by six windows, three on each story, with two smaller windows on each side and ornamental brick trim. It was constructed by the Guilford Building Company for $175,000 and could seat a thousand people.

Opening night was January 8, 1921, with *Food for Scandal,* starring Wanda Hawley. Manager William E. Stumpf no doubt welcomed his new patrons into the comfortable ivory and old rose interior. There was also a balcony, an organ, and a house orchestra. Later that same year, the Apollo was purchased by the Rome Organization.

After closing its doors to moviegoers in the late 1970s, the Apollo sat vacant until it was purchased by the Baltimore Tabernacle of Prayer in 1982. Time and neglect had taken their toll on the interior, necessitating extensive renovations to transform it from theater to church, but the exterior remains as it was constructed. Though now covered by a coat of paint, the original windows over the marquee are intact.

Under its new ownership, the Apollo serves the community in a different way, but the building also reminds the neighborhood residents of its wonderful past, when movie theaters in Baltimore were in their prime.

Many a golfing enthusiast has probably looked up while playing and seen these neatly maintained rowhouses across from the Clifton Park Golf Course on Harford Road. The obvious care of their owners is evident in the distinctive turret, roofline trim, and awnings.

From 1916 to 1948, the first tee of this pioneer municipal golf course was very near Harford Road, causing great difficulties for nearby residents and transit company vehicles. The course was laid out by Alexander Campbell on the grounds of Clifton, the estate of Johns Hopkins, who originally envisioned the area as the site for his university. Nearly twenty years after Hopkins' death, however, the grounds and mansion were acquired by the city of Baltimore from the university's trustees as part of the public park system.

The original mansion house was built in 1802–3 by Henry Thompson in the Georgian style of rough cast stone.

After purchasing the estate in 1836 for his summer home, Johns Hopkins extensively remodeled it in the Italian villa style, adding long arcades, Roman arches, light-colored stucco exterior walls, and a lofty tower. Today the mansion house serves as headquarters for Civic Works, a local youth program. The park has a golf course, tennis courts, picnic areas, and a nearby swimming pool.

Finding the Charm in Charm City

The builder of this tiny garage could easily have made it a plain square box but chose instead to give it character and charm. Perched at the edge of the sidewalk on Harford Road in the Herring Run Park area, it is a fine example of the beauty of symmetry and simplicity of design.

The stream channels of Chinquapin Run, Moore's Run, and Herring Run come together to form one of three major watersheds in the city. Herring Run, according to local folklore, was so named because it was a favorite spawning ground for the toothy fish. Much of the land for the park was purchased between 1908 and 1926, and it included parts of several estates on either side of Harford Road. Near here, where Hillen Road meets Harford Road, was one of the tollgates along the Harford Turnpike, as well as the estate of Henry Thompson, president of the Baltimore and Harford Turnpike Company.

This Florentine-lettered sign has been a well-known landmark in the Hamilton community since the theater was opened in early 1928 by Fred Schmuff, a film buyer for the Frank H. Durkee Enterprises chain of movie houses. The Arcade was built where a block of garages once stood, so it was separated from the main block by an alley. To solve this unique situation, a lobby area served as the bridge over the alley.

Talking pictures did not arrive until late in 1928, so the Arcade had a $12,000 Kilgen organ to provide music for the silent films. Although not palatial, the theater was well maintained and extremely respectable, with well-cleaned carpets, vases filled with artificial flowers, and men's and ladies' lounges. When talking pictures arrived, the organ was removed and the Arcade underwent its first renovation. On the bill that October 2 was *Lilac Time*, with Colleen Moore and Gary Cooper.

The Arcade's movie days came to an end on March 15, 1979, after the final performance of *Bermuda Triangle*, when the theater was closed by Tim Rosenberger, who had once been Frank Durkee's messenger boy and had gone on to become the Arcade's final manager. The offices for Durkee Enterprises continue to occupy the Arcade building.

Yard art has always been popular in Baltimore, and passing motorists along Northern Parkway near Harford Road have been treated to this immaculately maintained front yard for many years. The people who live here show their care by how well they tend this sombreroed figure and his donkey, keeping the grass well trimmed and the house neatly painted. While the scene may not be everyone's choice for yard decor, it adds a note of beauty and shows a resident's devotion to this neighborhood.

TWELVE

Belair Road

Another of the important turnpikes out of Baltimore was Belair Road, which begins as an extension of Gay Street in the city and runs in a northeasterly direction to the town of Bel Air in Harford County. In 1841 it was operated by the Baltimore and Jerusalem Turnpike Company, so named because the road led directly to the village of Jerusalem on the Little Gunpowder River, where a David Lee had a flour mill. Reportedly, Lee's Quaker grandfather, who was also named David Lee, made flintlocks for George Washington's army during the Revolutionary War.

In later years, Belair Road was known as Perry Hall Road, named for the community through which it travels. It is now part of the eastern section of U.S. Route 1 as it passes through Maryland on its way north to Maine.

As mentioned in the preface, this building is now vacant, but for decades the sleek, clean-looking geometric facade beckoned regular customers to come in for coffee, good inexpensive food, and the day's news. Originally built to face Belair Road, the White Tower was moved in the early 1950s to its present location to make way for a bank. Its glory days were during the years when Howard Street was the main shopping district and the Baltimore Colts were at their peak—following the 1958 championship game. In 1995, director Jodie Foster used the White Tower restaurant in some of her scenes for the movie *Home for the Holidays.*

When Gunther Benz began his upholstering business twenty-four years ago at this location on Belair Road, he decided to build a dramatic storefront so that people passing by could see the quality of his work. Some of the items on display belong to customers and are waiting to be picked up. Other pieces are for sale after having been carefully re-upholstered by Benz and his staff. The featured furniture is rotated at least once a week, so there are always new items to be seen and appreciated.

Definitely not a typical door decoration, this wolf clad in chains glares out at traffic as it passes by the Belair Sports Bar in the Little Flower community on Belair Road. The meaning of this unhappy creature is not known, but he definitely commands the attention of those who glance in his direction.

Motorists traveling along Belair Road can easily miss seeing this tiny barber shop. Not much larger than the width of a parking space, Fred's Barber Shop has been doing business in this location for the past forty-two years. From the neon in the window to the neatly folded awning to the sign that gives parking instructions, the meticulously maintained building reflects its owner's obvious pride and attention to detail.

Overlea

Before Belair Road crosses Interstate 695, it passes through the community of Overlea, which began as the result of the initiative of land developers who recognized that the area's high location was excellent for building purposes. In 1904, these businessmen persuaded United Railways to extend their car line further out Belair Road, promising it would be a profitable investment. Following this extension there was a great demand for lots. Seeing the value of the area, the Kennary Land Company and the Overlea Land Company took the lead in preparing the area for develop-

ment. Soon, hundreds of cottages appeared along the town's well-paved streets.

The town was first known as Lange's Farm, in honor of the family that owned a mansion and a large tract of land there. But as development continued, the area's topography contributed directly to the selection of a new name. Before the turn of the century, a person could stand on this high section of Belair Road and see miles of pastures. Another name for a pasture is a lea, so the name *Overlea* was chosen.

Inside this unusually decorated building on Belair Road in Overlea are more than twenty-five thousand hub caps, some dating to the early 1950s. Hub Cap City converted this former neighborhood grocery store fifteen years ago to accommodate its extensive inventory of hub caps and wheels. Not surprisingly, their motto is "Don't go around with your lug nuts showing." They also have locations on Crain Highway and Washington Boulevard.

This barber's pole hangs on the front of a shop in Belair Road in Overlea, where it serves to represent the long history of the profession. The Pyramids have yielded barbers' tools, and Alexander the Great's men shaved their faces so that the enemy could not grab their beards in battle. The profession was institutionalized in Ancient Greece where the cult of the barber-surgeon originated with the worship of Asclepius, the God of Medicine. Following the Roman invasion, the work of the barber-surgeon moved to the west and remained intact until the eighteenth century, when England's King George II separated the two fields.

In America, barbers were most active during the Colonial period, when most men were clean shaven. The Civil War era saw beards as the fashion, but after the war barber shops became permanent fixtures in most cities and towns. Besides offering a shave and a haircut, the barber would also pull teeth and, according to some reports, neuter tomcats.

All that remains today of the barber's surgical past are the colors on the pole: red for the blood, white for the bandages, and blue for the veins; the base represents the helmet of Don Quixote as well as the barber's basin.

Finding the Charm in Charm City

THIRTEEN

Route 40 East: Pulaski Highway

The background for the planning of Route 40 East in the mid-1920s began much earlier with another road that connected Baltimore and Philadelphia, a road that itself had begun as an Indian trail. Because of the natural topography, the Susquehannocks had chosen as their north-south route a compromise between the hazards of the marshes and estuaries of the Chesapeake Bay to the east and the steep hills and rugged terrain to the west. By 1685 the old Philadelphia Road was reasonably well laid out, and by 1690 the courts ordered it to be made passable for carts. After John Eager Howard surveyed the road in 1787, it quickly became an important traffic artery and post road, with stagecoach stops at Elkton, Charlestown, and Perryville. Because of the taverns and other comforts offered along the route, travelers once again chose to use the road instead of the Chesapeake Bay, and George Washington used it often to travel between Mount Vernon and Philadelphia.

As the road grew before the Civil War, the Pennsylvania Railroad roughly followed it, and later the B & O laid its tracks close beside the route. By 1923, citizens talked of improving the road, but it was 1931 before the State Roads Commission prepared plans to widen it, only to abandon the entire project when the legislature failed to approve the necessary bond issues. Four hundred petitions demanding widening of the road circulated in 1932, but Glenn L. Martin opposed the plan because he preferred a new route that more closely paralleled the Pennsylvania Railroad's tracks. Subsequently, the commission planned a dual-lane highway to Aberdeen, but the federal government had its own ideas and directed a new route of entry into Baltimore, thereby rejecting Maryland's plan completely and casting the old Philadelphia Road into oblivion.

Contracts for the first three-mile segment between Golden Ring and Cowenton were awarded in 1934. In January 1938, Governor Nice opened the Baltimore–Havre de Grace section, but the work was far from complete and was plagued for years by bickering and troubles. As early as the summer of 1940, the road was publicly admitted to be of poor design, due in part to an earlier decision that a full engineering survey would be too expensive. The concrete was beginning to crack, and members of the Philadelphia Road Non-Partisan Protective Association ridiculed the road, calling it the "Muskrat Trail" because the chosen route largely ran over the marshlands inhabited by those creatures.

Even the highway's name brought dissension and disagreement. The state proudly erected signs naming it "Nice Highway" in honor of the governor who had opened it, but they were taken down by the federal government, who claimed that it was against regulations to name a federal highway for a living person. Maryland's legislature met and finally chose to name the highway for General Casimir Pulaski, a Revolutionary War hero.

Until 1963, Route 40 was the highway used to travel from Baltimore to New Jersey, but the opening of Interstate 95 changed that, and Route 40 nearly died in the late 1960s. Beginning as Orleans Street, then changing to Pulaski Highway where it joins Fayette Street, the Route 40 East of today provides a nostalgic look at the earlier years of auto travel and remains a favorite route for those motorists who prefer its less hectic pace.

This well-known art deco sign, complete with neon, hangs outside one of the more famous "strip theaters" on East Baltimore Street, better known in Baltimore as "the Block." The club was opened in 1936 by Solomon Goodman and his wife, but its more famous owner was Blaze Starr.

Born Fannie Belle Fleming in the early 1930s in New-ground Hollow near Wilsondale, West Virginia, Blaze began performing in her late teens and came to the 2 O'Clock Club in December 1950. Soon Mr. Goodman became her personal manager, and he eventually sold her the club in 1968. Over the next four years, Ms. Starr worked to elevate the reputation of the Block by providing family-type shows and continued to perform her own parody of a striptease, finally selling the club in 1972. At that time, the building also housed a burlesque theater, an envelope factory, a violin factory, and a gypsy shop.

Hungry residents and visitors to the area around Johns Hopkins Hospital have been stopping at this family-owned restaurant on Broadway for more than thirty years. Originally called Maria's, the name was changed to Mamma Mia's in the late 1960s, when this perky chef and sign were painted. Patrons are welcome to dine in or carry out from the wide selection of foods offered by the busy staff that works here.

The dramatic art deco lines of this building, known for more than fifty years as Luby Chevrolet, were added when the original structure was remodeled in the mid-1940s. Although the owners had been in business since purchasing an existing dealership in 1938, after World War II they decided to take advantage of the shape of the existing building, and they engaged the services of architect Harry Katz for the job. Because their original neon sign was plainly visible from the trains that passed nearby, the owners wanted to add more neon as part of the new design. Katz won an award for the project, and Baltimore gained one of its best-loved buildings.

In the early 1990s, Ron Clancy of the KCM architectural firm oversaw the remodeling of the building for a second time. The owners of Luby Chevrolet sold the building in 1994 but continued to rent it, finally closing the business in 1996.

Eastern Avenue

From a waterfront beginning at President Street between Little Italy and Fells Point, Eastern Avenue travels east through Highlandtown before turning northeast over the Back River and through the Essex and Middle River communities to its final destination at Gunpowder Falls State Park, east of Chase.

In 1899 the state made a geological survey of its 14,482 miles of roads. At that time, more than 13,000 miles were dirt, almost 900 miles were stone, over 200 miles were gravel, and 250 miles were of shell, with Eastern Avenue being the most important shell road out of Baltimore. In those early years, roads were made of the best available materials, and the tidewater region of Baltimore County had an abundance of oyster shells. It is no surprise that Baltimore County also had the most roads with this surface. Shell roads, which were found to be more serviceable than roads of other surfaces, were formed by merely throwing down whole oyster shells and allowing wagon wheels and animal hooves to crush them in place.

Eastern Avenue gave access to the popular shores and

resins in the lower end of Baltimore County, where many a turn-of-the-century politician liked to host oyster roasts. When the State Roads Commission was formed in 1908, shell roads, which could be very dusty in windy conditions, were falling out of favor; as the automobile traffic continued to increase, hard surface roads were preferred.

During Prohibition, a person seeking an evening's entertainment could take a fourteen-cent ride on the old #23 line out Eastern Avenue to the area of the Back River and find a source for gambling, slot machines, bootleg liquor, and other forbidden diversions.

Although part of the road is named Eastern Boulevard, because of its higher design standards, the entire length is more commonly known as Eastern Avenue. Today it serves a wide diversity of residential, commercial, and light industrial communities while still remaining a major route to the Gunpowder Falls State Park and other beach-front parks nearby, which attract visitors from the entire Baltimore region.

Little Italy

When the traffic patterns were reversed on Lombard and Pratt Streets in 1975, the owner of Pastore's Italian Foods decided to clarify the direction. His solution was to use the stark rear wall of his own building for this mural and artistically show the way to Albemarle Street. Utilizing a classic trompe l'oeil (fool the eye) technique, he made the blank wall appear to be a building with windows and flourishing ivy. Not only did he accomplish his task of giving bewildered motorists useful directions, he also enhanced

the general atmosphere of the neighborhood while tying the rear wall in with the red, white, and green decoration of the rest of his building.

The neighborhood of Little Italy, which occupies fifteen square blocks, was settled in the mid-1850s. Some of the first Italians to buy houses were sailors from Genoa or adventurers with gold fever who had been bound for California but decided instead to stay and settle the waterfront around the President Street Station. Soon this passenger terminal was surrounded by small hostelries operated by these early Italian residents. As word of their good fortune spread to family and friends back home, hundreds of people from Naples, Abruzzi, Cefalù, and Palermo began arriving. In 1880, Cardinal Gibbons laid the cornerstone of St. Leo's Church, which is regarded as the spiritual, social, and physical center of the community.

Delicious food has always been the backbone of dining in Little Italy, and this brick facade hides the food manufacturing business that has grown out of the family restaurant across the street.

Now run by Frank Vellegia Sr., his brother, and their children, the original restaurant was begun in 1937 by the brothers' parents, both first-generation immigrants from the old country. Frank's father settled first in Atlantic City, where he repaired the boardwalk before becoming an apprentice to a stonemason. When he moved to Baltimore, he continued to work as a stonemason when he could, but the Great Depression made finding such work difficult. Frank's mother worked with her sisters as a seamstress and tailor. When the couple married, they decided to use their savings to open a small restaurant where their friends could meet. While Mrs. Vellegia prepared the food during the day, Mr. Vellegia worked and helped out at the restaurant in the evenings. Today, the restaurant seats two hundred fifty people and is the oldest continually owned restaurant in the area.

In the 1970s, the family decided to make their pasta products available and opened the manufacturing plant. They employ longtime local residents who carefully prepare the recipes that have been handed down over the years. The majority of the products are handmade, but increasing demand has led to the addition of a few machines, handpicked from Italy. In addition to various sheet egg pastas, such as linguine and fettucini, the company prepares sauces and filled pasta dishes, which are available at their retail counter or sold wholesale to restaurants, hotels, and supermarkets.

Fells Point

This diverse waterfront community owes its start to two English Quaker brothers who settled east of the Jones Falls in 1726. Edward Fell, one of the early large landholders, kept a store. His brother, William, built a house on what is now Lancaster Street and opened a shipyard on a tract of land then called Copus's Harbor, known after 1730 as Fells Point. Other shipbuilders soon joined him, and a public wharf was constructed. Larger ships, which could not enter the shallower basin up the Patapsco at Baltimore Town, could navigate the Point's deeper waters and discharge their cargo, immigrants, or indentured servants. Later, during the Revolutionary War, ships there embarked Continental troops as well.

In 1763 William's son, Col. Edward Fell, laid out the town, giving the streets solidly English names. The wealthy residents built their homes along Market Street (now Broadway) and land speculators, not knowing whether Baltimore Town or "The Point" was the better place to invest, bought properties in both. In 1781, the assembly annexed the eighty acres that included Fells Point, thus making it part of Baltimore Town.

Fells Point has always looked to the sea. Here were found shipyards, rigging lofts, and ship chandlers' stores. Crews from the many ships that sailed to and from the area founded Sailortown, which extended along Thames Street from Bond to Wolfe Streets and featured boardinghouses with home-cooked meals. This neighborhood of working people also enjoyed a variety of taverns and dance halls, complete with sand-sprinkled floors.

Ships were the business of the day, with sloops and ketches and a twenty-gun frigate, the *Virginia,* launched here as the first warship of the Continental Navy. But the region's specialty was the Baltimore Clipper, a swift topsail schooner with raking masts, little rigging, and a low freeboard. During the Revolutionary War, some two hundred and fifty privateers were fitted out, with another one hundred twenty-six following in the War of 1812. One of the larger and handsomer clipper ships was the *Anne McKim,* built in 1833 for Baltimore merchant Isaac McKim by the Kennard & Williamson shipyard. She featured a copper-sheathed bottom and Spanish mahogany trim.

Today, with the continuing renaissance of Baltimore's extensive waterfront, the older buildings of Fells Point are being converted to condominiums, apartments, restaurants, shops, and offices, all of which serve to attract a multitude of visitors eager to enjoy the many activities of this historic waterfront community.

In 1968, when Lauren and Tony Norris married and moved to Baltimore from Washington, D.C., they had no idea that one day they would own and operate Bertha's, one of Fells Point's most popular dining spots. He was a classical guitarist, she was a violinist, and both were content to teach and to perform whenever possible. But a serious illness in 1971 marked the end of teaching for Lauren. At the same time, a friend discovered the old Lone Star Bar in Fells Point and thought it would be fun to run it. He asked the Norrises if they would like to join him and play their music in the back room. This idea really appealed to them, so they pitched in their savings and finalized the deal in 1972.

All went well until they were summoned to appear before the Liquor Board for a violation. Unknown to them, in 1971 the law had been changed and live music was no longer allowed where liquor was served. Area merchants had pressured the city because of fears that the strip theaters on the Block, which were using live bands at the time, might spread to Fells Point. Had the Norrises known of the change when it happened, they could have been grandfathered in, but then there would be no restaurant.

As it happened, they had an empty back room until an artist they knew, who had been a chef at Martick's Restaurant, offered to help them start a restaurant. On that opening night in 1974 they were swamped, and Lauren, more than seven months pregnant, was close to tears wondering how they would handle all the people. Business remained steady, allowing them to open their second dining room in 1980. But the bar and restaurant still did not have a good name.

In an effort to create a better and more attractive atmosphere, the Norrises moved in some antique collectibles, including several stained glass windows, which they hung from the ceiling and illuminated. One of these bore the name of Bertha E. Bartholomew, so someone suggested they name the place Bertha's, which they did. No one knew anything about Bertha, but that didn't seem to matter.

Following a public interest newspaper article that mentioned the window, a great-niece of Bertha's surfaced. She and her husband, residents of California, were visiting Bertha's old South Baltimore neighborhood and had gone to her church only to find that it had been replaced by a modern structure. Following the necessary six-month advertising for the sale of consecrated items, the church had sold the window to a junk dealer, which was how Tony Norris had discovered it. Bertha had been a teacher of elocution and piano to children in South Baltimore. Fortunately, Bertha's great-niece left the window with its present owners.

Today, Bertha's continues to serve the many regular and visiting customers plates of steaming mussels and other culinary delights at the sign of the girl in the swing, the third in a series created by artists over the last twenty-five years.

Located high above the street at the corner of Broadway and Shakespeare Street is this fading reminder of a "noble experiment" in this country's history that failed. In short, prohibition made illegal the manufacture, sale, and transportation of intoxicating liquors for beverage purposes.

During the first decade of the twentieth century, small groups of "drys" active in Baltimore's temperance movement met and chanted favorite hymns declaring that Maryland was going dry. While their actions annoyed area distillers and brewers, they were not considered a serious threat. But the outbreak of World War I gave them an easy opportunity to convince the public of the need to protect the morals of the soldiers in camp. On midnight of June 30, 1919, postwar prohibition went into effect. With the exception of 2.75 percent beer (affectionately known as "near beer"), the legal sale of alcoholic beverages ceased in Baltimore and the United States. Following this victory, the Anti-Saloon League further campaigned to end the evil of drink forever. With the Eighteenth Amendment to the Constitution, which Herbert Hoover described as "noble in motive and far-reaching in purpose," campaigners thought they had succeeded.

However, local support was lackluster, at best. Maryland had no enforcement law of its own to back up the national Volstead Act, and Baltimore, with a longstanding history of brewing and beer gardens, was decidedly "wet" in its opinions. Large wooded sections of Harford and Cecil Counties as well as Southern Maryland provided excellent opportunities for the illegal manufacture of liquor, and the term *bootlegger* became a common word.

In time, the dictatorial attitude of the "dry" leaders and the tyrannical behavior of the agents charged with enforcing the law disgusted Maryland's heretofore neutral citizens. The *Evening Sun* newspaper adopted an antiprohibition policy, methodically embarrassing local candidates by asking if they were wet or dry, a campaign that helped create and popularize the phrase "Maryland Free State." But the antiprohibition movement gained considerably more support when the rapidly escalating gangsterism associated with the law led to murder and the kidnapping of children.

Finally, after fourteen years, the "noble experiment" ended at midnight on April 6, 1933, when 75,000 glasses of beer were consumed in Baltimore and the members of the Association Against the Prohibition Amendment stood victorious.

This aging brick building on Jackson's Wharf in Fells Point serves as a reminder of the years when shipping was a major activity on Thames Street. Known as the "sawtooth" building because it has a sawtooth design when viewed from the waterfront, it served in the 1920s and 1930s as the corporate headquarters for Rukert Terminals, Inc., a stevedoring and warehousing company founded in 1921 by two brothers, W. G. N. "Cap" and George Rukert. As part of their expansion, they purchased a series of buildings along Thames Street, including those on Brown's Wharf, Miller's Wharf, Chase's Wharf, and Jackson's Wharf.

The original buildings date to the early 1820s, when they were used for storing flour and cotton to be exported to Europe and coffee imported from South America. In 1840 George Brown, son of Irish immigrant Alexander Brown, bought the property, using it to help build the financial empire of Alex. Brown & Sons. The warehouses were enlarged in 1868 and were operated for a time by a Joseph Bias. The Western Maryland Railway then purchased them,

and finally sold them to Rukert Terminals, Inc.

Finding that the older multilevel warehouses were no longer practical because of their size and lack of elevators, the company sold these buildings and moved to the Canton area. Now in its fourth generation of ownership, Rukert Terminals occupies one hundred acres and four piers on Clinton Street and ranks as one of the largest ports of call in Baltimore.

Located at waterside on Thames Street, this beautifully painted entryway has helped to bring national exposure to Baltimore in recent years as part of the set for Barry Levinson's network television series, *Homicide: Life on the Streets.* On the site of the building used for the make-believe police headquarters once stood a small village; in 1912 it was demolished to make way for a cargo pier. In order to make up to the community for the loss of the village, the city opened the recreation pier in 1914. Among its various facilities is a ballroom, which served for many years as the meeting place for the young people of Fells Point's diverse ethnic groups.

Today the pier is part of the city's Recreation and Parks Department, but it remains active in the maritime community as home base for the tugboats and offices of the Moran Towing Company of Maryland. Because it serves as film studios for the television series, the pier has helped renew interest in Fells Point, and it is a highlight on many tourists' lists of places to see when visiting Baltimore.

Since the late 1970s, landlubbers and sailors alike have delighted in visiting this Fells Point shop, filled to overflowing with curiosities of the seven seas. Situated on the Ann Street Wharf, its third location since opening, this adventuring shop is run by Steve Bunker, a former merchant marine from upstate Maine who gave up his life at sea to settle in this ethnically diverse maritime neighborhood. Over the years, he has worked hard to fill his building with everything nautical, including anchors for still-functioning ships, cannon, supplies for sailing ships, ships' nameboards, the uniforms of various navies, and tribal art from South America and the African coast. The diver's suit hails from the South China Sea, where it was retired after taking the lives of two people. In addition to dealing in ships' supplies and collectibles, Bunker also does a lot of salvage work, and he can still deliver large sailing ships.

In keeping with the life of a sailor, two macaws also inhabit the store, and occasionally one will accompany its owner to one of the area's saloons, which operate as neighborhood city halls. On one such foray to the Cat's Eye Pub, Bunker and his macaw were greeted by the resident bar parrot, a monkey, and several dogs. When a fight broke out between the dogs, patrons were seen jumping over the bar to get out of the way of the angry animals.

In addition to running his nautical trading company, Bunker also serves as president of the community association, which continues to play an active role in preserving the buildings and history of this vibrant waterfront community.

In the midst of this busy section of Fleet Street, this distinctive storefront stands out in contrast to the surrounding businesses. Dating to the mid-1930s, when the store opened, this painted metal sign is typical of the clean lines associated with the art deco period. Before the family opened their appliance store, they operated a clothing shop from the same location, but they chose to redesign the storefront to mark the beginning of their new venture.

For people who grew up in Fells Point, "Meet me under the pig" was a common way of fixing a spot to rendezvous. This hanging pink porker also marks the location of a butcher shop that dates to the 1920s, when Joe Siemek and his family opened their business here. Hours were long in those years, starting at six in the morning and going until midnight. At the height of his business, Joe had twelve clerks, three butchers, and all ten family children working at the store. At that time, bulk food items such as rice came in large barrels, and the children spent their time breaking the shipments down into smaller packages. The shop also supplied veal to Haussner's before they opened their large restaurant on Eastern Avenue. Although it is missing its glowing neon lights, the hanging pig continues to serve as a distinctive landmark on this busy stretch of Fleet Street in Fells Point.

This building in Fells Point is a particularly fine example of the "art" of Formstone, the hand-sculptured covering for the facades of brick rowhouses. Invented in Baltimore by Albert Knight, who received a patent for it in 1937, Formstone was manufactured by an offshoot of Lasting Products, a Baltimore paint manufacturing company. Especially popular in the 1950s and 1960s, Formstone is installed onto expanded metal lath, which is anchored into the brick or mortar joints on sixteen-inch centers. After the lath is given a base coat of cement stucco, the cookie-cutter-like molds are filled with colored stucco and applied over the wet basecoat, some in a more animated fashion than others.

Lasting Products even had a school where workers from all over the country were trained to apply this material to wood and other surfaces in order to give the appearance of natural stone structures. The original Formstone Company went out of business in 1963, but other companies continued to supply it under such names as Dixie Stone, Permastone, Romanstone, and Modernstone. Still available today, Formstone is either loved or detested and, once installed, can be difficult to remove.

The Atlantic Southwestern Broom Company, in operation until 1989, when the business was sold to the O'Cedar Company, was begun in 1907 by August Rosenberger in the Canton area south of Eastern Avenue. It recalls the time when this area was devoted to industry.

In the 1850s, Rosenberger emigrated from Prussia, first settling in New Orleans, Louisiana, and later moving to Evansville, Indiana, where he started a hardware business. When a customer who owed him money left him a broom machine instead, he decided to make brooms to sell in his store. Before long, he was also making brooms for other companies in the area. Having done well with the enterprise, he was able to donate the money needed to rebuild the local Catholic church, which had been destroyed by fire. His business continued to flourish, and he soon had plants in Oakland, California, and Wichita, Kansas. When he moved to Baltimore, he bought out the Custom Broom and Brush Company, which operated out of the prison, and began constructing this first of seven building sections to house the growing concern. Knowing the extreme flammability of broom-making materials, Rosenberger made sure each section was made of double brick with connecting fire doors, so that if any one section caught fire, the others would be protected.

The Little Lady broom was sold exclusively to the A & P Company, which accounted for 65 percent of Rosenberger's business at one time. The Little Nugget was a top quality broom that sported a gold finish, had a fancy run-down (or decorative spiral) on the handle, and used the finest quality broom corn. At the height of production, the company employed three hundred workers and produced

3.6 million brooms in a single year.

During World War I, the Wichita plant was used to manufacture aircraft. In time, the other plants were also sold and the business was consolidated in Baltimore. According to older residents of the area, the plant was known as "Canton College" during World War II because employees received draft deferments for working there.

Stories also circulate about the plant being haunted by the founder's ghost.

behind his back, a perfect description of August Rosenberger, who had been dead for fifteen years. After that, the engineer always turned on all the lights while tending the boiler.

When the broom business was sold, the family, now in its fourth generation, retained the building. Today great-grandson Scott Rosenberger is converting the historic structure in the rediscovered Canton area to a multiuse space, with plans for offices and an Internet center.

This decorative little brick structure in the Polish community south of Eastern Avenue brings to mind the Bailey Building and Loan in the 1947 movie *It's a Wonderful Life.* Like the movie version, this real-life thrift institution represents the care and pride of a neighborhood.

Prior to the Civil War, Polish immigrants began arriving along with Czechs and Germans, and they decided to stay and work instead of moving on across the country. They were employed in steel mills and factories and continued to preserve the traditions of the old country. Most important among their values was to be thrifty and to save money in order to purchase a home.

A souvenir program celebrating the restoration of Poland proudly states that the Polish Building and Loan Association, under the leadership of William Karwacki, paid 6 percent on savings twice a year. In 1928, with the help of some fifteen Polish building and loan associations with assets of $10 million, 75 percent of the Poles in Baltimore owned their own homes.

One early morning when few lights were on, the engineer charged with starting the factory's coal-fired steam boiler thought he saw an old man down the hall. When he called to him, the man disappeared. Later in the day, the engineer told another worker about seeing an old man wearing glasses hunched over with his hands

Located a few blocks south on Dundalk Avenue, The Circle was the favorite meeting place of area teens during the 1950s and 1960s. On July 3, 1947, Francis and Helen Gretz opened the perfectly round, white concrete diner, which was designed by architect Harry Wills. More than a thousand orange flashing bulbs spelled out "Bar-B-Q" and the elevated sandwich-shaped sign revolved until a windstorm ruined the motor.

When it opened, The Circle was the only place in Baltimore to offer carry-out and eat-in service. During the restaurant's fifty years of operation, the menu remained small and included sweet pork barbecue, the "Cheese E Q" (a barbecue sandwich with cheese), hamburgers, cheeseburgers, cheese steaks, and thick homemade milkshakes. Because The Circle was open from six P.M. to three A.M., many customers began their evenings there and returned in the early morning hours for hand-dipped ice cream before calling it a night.

After his wife died in 1974, Gretz continued to operate the restaurant until July 1997, when advancing age and a broken hip forced him to close. The prospects for the restaurant reopening are slim at best, and the landmark may be lost to the wrecking ball.

Dundalk

Southeast of Eastern Avenue is the community of Dundalk, an area that remained quietly undiscovered until the outbreak of World War I.

In the mid-1800s, Henry McShane chose the area for his bell foundry and named the site, which was little more than a rail junction for his mill, after his birthplace in Ireland. Farming remained the main occupation of the area until 1916, when World War I prompted Bethlehem Steel, which operated at Sparrows Point to the south, to build a town for its workers.

The Dundalk Company, a subsidiary of Bethlehem Steel, purchased a thousand acres of land for the community, which was laid out by the company that developed Roland Park, the first planned community in the United States. Indeed, developers even described Dundalk as the "workmen's Roland Park." The establishment of Fort Holabird greatly increased the need for housing for the shipbuilders and defense workers, so an agency of the U.S. Shipping Board sent in workers to construct a picturesque enclave of English style homes, laid out appropriately in the shape of a ship, with street names such as Arrowship and Flagship Roads and Admiral Boulevard.

The need for security prompted the government to surround the community with barbed wire and sentry posts, creating a forbidden city to those not presenting the required credentials. Following the end of the war and the relaxation of these security regulations, the barbed wire was removed, but hard times put a crimp in the area's expansion plans. Renewed interest surfaced in 1924, but the original plan had by then been laid aside, and over the intervening years layers of unplanned development surrounded the original community. Efforts are under way to redefine the ambiance of Dundalk as it was intended when originally planned.

Built in the graceful art deco style with its formed metal crown of shells, this corner store spent much of its life serving the Dundalk community as Eddie's Food Market, one of the many grocery stores operated by Edward A. Levy, a longtime resident of Dundalk. Levy began his business in 1927 with a tiny grocery store in Sparrows Point, eventually expanding the chain to include twenty-one supermarkets in the area before selling it to Integro, Inc., in 1956.

When the food market closed, Goodwill Industries leased the building for an outlet store. Then they moved to a nearby location, and the Salvation Army leased the building as one of its thrift stores, where used clothing, furniture, and appliances are sold to support the organization's activities.

The Salvation Army came to Baltimore in October 1880, a year after the first branch had opened in the United States. The organization was founded in London in 1865 by William Booth, a former Methodist minister, and was known as the Hallelujah Army until 1878. Booth, whose motto was "Soup, soap and salvation," traveled throughout England as a revivalist, proclaiming his belief that a man should be fed before he could learn religion. The first "soldiers" who came to America began their work in the Hampden community and spread throughout the area serving the causes of the organization.

Any lover of model trains would probably screech to a halt at this Dundalk shop, the only one of its kind in that community. French's Trains and Hobbies dates to 1904, the year of the Great Baltimore Fire, when Howard French, a pioneer in the bicycle and motorcycle field, and Warren Wimmer opened for business on the corner of Baltimore and Howard Streets. Their store's five floors were filled with a wide variety of sporting goods, bicycles, fishing equipment, and, of course, trains. At one time, French's supplied motorcycles to the Baltimore Police Department. In the 1930s, it became an authorized Lionel train dealer and service station, a tradition that continues today.

Following Howard French's retirement in 1949, Warren Wimmer and his son Warren continued to operate the business. When the elder Wimmer died, his son devoted his life to the store until his own death, in 1978. Then the current owners, George Stanton and his partner, Harry Bellsinger, bought the shop and moved it to Conkling Street in Highlandtown, where its main business was trains.

Since moving to Dundalk in 1984, the shop has expanded three times and has added general hobby items and model kits to its merchandise. Of the many memorable events that have happened at the store, one of the recent highlights was a private two-hour shopping spree for a young train-loving patient, compliments of the Make-A-Wish Foundation.

Highlandtown

The community of Highlandtown, once a town separate from Baltimore, is rich with the heritage of its early immigrant settlers. That history began in 1680 when John E. Hurst, described as a carefree innkeeper, could not pay the mortgage on his land and chose to assign it to Captain Richard Colgate, a wealthy Englishman. Colgate enlisted the help of the Susquehannock Indians and gradually worked the virgin land into fertile farms, which helped increase the number of settlers in the area. When Colgate died, in 1722, he left six thousand acres, which remained in his family until 1870.

Until the Civil War, prosperity grew with the addition of new businesses and horse racing at the Potter's Race Course. In October 1861, the federal government took over the race course section, and Fort Marshall was quickly constructed. During these years, the small village of Snake Hill evolved, but Conrad Schluderberg, a local butcher who wanted a name that would give the area a better image, formed a committee to select one. On the committee were his brothers Henry and William (also butchers), Henry Adam, a Mr. Elgert, Fred Heim, Theodore Maasch, and Conrad Schwind. They quickly rejected *Fort Marshall* and *Butcher's Hill*. After considering the high elevation of the area, *Highland Town* seemed the best choice, a name that eventually became Highlandtown.

Besides the slaughtering and meat businesses of the immigrant butchers, the village also had many breweries, including Vogel's on Eastern Avenue, Schlaffer's and Gunther's on Conkling Street, and the Bay View Brewer on Sixteenth, as well as Zimmerman's, Thau's, and the Monumental and National Companies. The streetcar made Highlandtown readily accessible, and the area's respectable family beer gardens drew many Sunday visitors from Baltimore, where stricter laws had closed saloons.

Corner stores, roadhouses, and family businesses of every description soon filled the growing village, which was finally absorbed by Baltimore in the years 1915–20. Amidst the busy traffic of today's Highlandtown, a visitor can pause at its highest point on Eastern Avenue to appreciate the panorama of the city below and imagine it at a time when the area was nothing but farmland.

Filled with memories long past, this corner store on Foster Avenue south of Eastern Avenue in the heart of Highlandtown was started by August Elberth, a butcher from Germany who worked for the Schluderberg company until he opened his own butcher shop in the late 1800s. He gradually added groceries, and his son joined him in the business. His granddaughter Gertrude described it as a "nice little corner store in a neighborhood where people knew each other." During their school years, she and her sister would take turns getting up at 4:15 on Saturday mornings so that they could be at the store when it opened to help bag groceries.

Before World War II, the store was open from five in the morning until ten or eleven at night, but during the war years, when meat was extremely scarce, it began to close at nine, then at eight, and finally at six. Gertrude's Uncle Mike had the three buildings next door, in which he ran a dry goods store, a shoe store, and a haberdashery. The buildings were all connected so customers could walk through from one to another, and upstairs one could find toys and a Santa Claus at Christmas.

Being a German parish, the nearby Sacred Heart of Jesus Church read the gospel in German, but the anti-German sentiment of World War II brought an end to that. After the war, Gertrude's father retired, and he sold the business in 1946. The new owner continued to operate it for more than twenty years before he also retired. Now a private residence, the building, with its simple and elegant art deco facade, remains a graceful link to the rich history of the early immigrant families in Baltimore.

Originally founded in 1953, this nonprofit men's social club of sixty active members has been a neighborhood fixture on this quiet corner since the early 1960s. The building, located a few blocks south of Eastern Avenue, was originally a savings and loan association when the club purchased it, and it now provides a convenient place for members to gather and exchange the news of the day. The club, named for one of the twenty founding members, sponsors events such as an annual golf tournament in order to support community charities.

Not many shops can claim to have inspired a movie set, but this offbeat landmark can. When area filmmaker John Waters was preparing to shoot his 1988 movie *Hairspray*, the uniquely adorned Lucky Three Dog and Cat Grooming inspired the fictitious Hardy Har Har joke shop run by Trudy Turnblatt's father, played by actor Jerry Stiller.

Since the late 1970s, area neighbors have been treated to three different sets of murals. The earliest pooch portraits were replaced in 1982 by other poses of perky pets, which remained until 1991, when peeling paint dictated their removal. During the intervening years, when the walls remained undecorated, some of owner David Walter's neighbors thought he had gone out of business. But in 1995 he began the always difficult task of selecting new pet poses. Now when residents stroll past the corner of Fleet and Conkling Streets, they once again find amusing views of the owner's favorite four-legged friends.

When this theater first opened, in 1914, Highland-town was not yet a part of Baltimore, and Conkling Street, where the Grand is located, was known as Third Street. Although it was a legitimate stage theater at the time, complete with curtains and a seventy-five-foot-high flytrap, it was being used for motion pictures. Frank Durkee added it to his stable of theaters in 1921, but the theater's interior was not extensively remodeled until 1926.

A new foot-thick concrete floor was installed to separate the theater from the cattle pens, which had been used by the Philipp Wagner slaughterhouse, beneath it. August Nolte, who was managing the Grand at the time, only went next door once to see the butcher's operation. When a workman wanted to tie a new concession stand into the foundation, he chiseled a hole in the floor, only to lose his crowbar to the cattle pens below. He never retrieved it. Following the makeover, the Grand reopened on September 11, 1926, with the feature film *Bigger than Barnum,* starring Viola Dana and Ralph Lewis.

Frank Durkee was an inventive and energetic individual. After seeing moving pictures for the first time, he realized that he would have to take this new entertainment to the people, so in 1908, at the age of twenty, he strapped his equipment to his back and went from hall to hall. In his early years, when he owned the Paradise at Washington and Federal Streets, he did everything from taking the tickets and singing behind the screen (until someone complained) to bidding customers farewell as they left after the show. He joined forces in 1916 with Charles E. Nolte, who operated the Linwood, and C. W. Pacy, who operated the Garden on South Charles Street. By 1921 they had added

eight theaters, including the Grand and the Patterson in Highlandtown. Over the next fifty years, their empire grew to contain forty-one movie houses in the area, making it the largest and one of the oldest movie circuits in Baltimore.

The Grand had its share of troubles during its years of operation. In 1928, nine hundred people were evacuated during a fire, and another fire hit in 1943 necessitating the evacuation of three hundred and fifty patrons. The theater was robbed in September of that same year. Neighborhood residents continued to enjoy

movies at the Grand until the mid-1980s, when the doors closed for the final time, leaving the blank marquee as a haunting reminder of the glory days of the past.

While many people in Baltimore decorate their windows for the holidays, this window on Highland Avenue appears to be of a more permanent nature, reflecting the resident's obvious love of white glazed ceramic figurines. Cleverly disguised coffee cans covered in aluminum foil serve as supports for the shelves, and the floral patterned lace curtains provide the perfect backdrop for this carefully arranged grouping of cherished objects.

Since at least the late 1940s, there has been a neighborhood tavern on this corner south of Patterson Park, and this latest incarnation has been serving patrons since 1987. Named for the owner, this well-maintained establishment reflects the care and pride of this East Baltimore community. The unusual black and green vitrine glass tile is an attractive and dramatic contrast to other buildings nearby.

When neighborhood residents need a new appliance, they often stop in at this distinctively curved corner building on Eastern Avenue. Before 1946, the Bolewicki family operated a real estate office out of an older building on this site, but they decided to demolish it and build a new home for this appliance business. They engaged the services of Sam Kroll, who had built a similar building a few blocks away. Originally, the site of the Bolewickis' shop was home to an ear, nose, and throat hospital.

Finding the Charm in Charm City

While most movie theater signs were changed to horizontal displays when their marquees were redesigned, this grand, lighted vertical sign continues to dominate the corner in Highlandtown where the Patterson operated for more than sixty-five years, providing entertainment to the residents of the area.

The original Patterson, which opened in 1910, was an open-air theater with an indoor theater next to it. After spending the Roaring Twenties as a dance hall, it was purchased by Gilbert Pacy in 1929 for Durkee Enterprises and almost completely demolished. In his redesign of the theater, John Zink chose an oriental theme, with an interior color scheme of red, orange, and gold with matching draperies. Lighting was provided by ornate crystal chandeliers, and the seating was expanded to accommodate twelve hundred people. Because the Patterson was built over an ancient sandbar from the time when the early harbor reached to the Highlandtown area, piles were driven deep into the ground to support the building.

Following its reconstruction by the E. Eyring & Son Company, builders of many other area theaters, the Patterson reopened on September 26, 1930, with the feature film *Queen High*, starring Charles Ruggles. Sound equipment was added in 1932. Always aware of the value of public relations, manager Albert Nolte installed a sign over the door which read: "Through these portals walk the most beautiful girls in the world."

In the early 1980s, the theater lost its grand movie house atmosphere when it was divided to accommodate two

smaller screens. Following a gradual decline in business, the Patterson closed its doors on December 28, 1995, thereby closing the book on the reign of Durkee Enterprises in the movie business.

Fishermen from near and far have been shopping for bait and tackle at this third-generation family business on Eastern Avenue since 1915. The shop actually began as a confectionery where Anna Tochterman sold sweets. When the soft crabs that her husband, Thomas, brought home from his job at the Baltimore Fish Market sold well as bait, they replaced the candy with hooks, sinkers, and bloodworms.

In 1938, the tackle shop passed to sons Tommy Jr. and Edward, who enlarged the small family business dramatically. While Edward chose to concentrate on the wholesale market, Tommy ran the shop. Even though it was open from five A.M. to eleven P.M., seven days a week, Tommy and his wife, Antoinette, who lived upstairs, were often awakened by Fells Point bar patrons who wanted to go fishing, regardless of the hour.

The leaping fish neon sign was created in the 1950s and refurbished in the early 1990s by the original designer. Today, Thomas and Anna's grandson Tony operates T. G. Tochterman and Sons, which is now the oldest family-run tackle business in the country. Its inventory, which includes everything from delicate fly-fishing gear to powerful deep sea equipment, continues to attract a large and loyal clientele of anglers.

For the better part of the nineteenth century, Baltimore was the leading importer of coffee in the United States, a trade that flourished thanks mainly to the desirability of Maryland's flour, which was sought by other countries because of its better keeping qualities. Nearby Brown's Wharf and Belt's Wharf were known as the coffee wharves, so Fells Point is the perfect place for this festive-looking coffee house.

Funk's Democratic Coffee cleverly combines elements of the names of two former occupants. Funk's Confectionery originally occupied the building, followed in the 1920s by the Polish American Democratic Club. During the 1960s, the PADC leased the building to an insurance agency. Then, on December 18, 1982, Funk's Democratic Coffee opened. The owner decided to brighten up the Formstone and the curb in front of the store by painting sections of each with rich vibrant colors, which carry over to the interior. Besides serving coffee seven days a week, Funk's also exhibits the work of local artists, offers live jazz on Thursday nights, and hosts the weekly meetings of *LINK*, the Baltimore Arts Journal.

Weary motorists driving in Fells Point are visually rewarded when they come to this spotlessly maintained house and yard on Eastern Avenue. Sporting Baltimore's classic Formstone, now painted a sparkling white, this typical area home is decorated with green and white striped awnings, which add to its overall impact.

While many awnings are now metal and permanently installed, the early awnings in Baltimore were made of the same canvas duck produced for ships' sails by the Mount Vernon Mills in Woodberry. Sail canvas was white, but for awnings the material was dyed a khaki color. In later years a mildew retardant turned it gray. Soon, lined patterns of striping were added in alternating green, khaki, white, and red.

Canvas would deteriorate in the winter weather, so the awnings were put up at the start of summer and removed at the end of the warm days for winter storage. Because they were supported by a metal pipe framework and ropes, one needed a certain degree of skill to put them up, so men would often go from door to door offering to do the job for a small fee.

Besides being decorative, when combined with window and ceiling fans awnings offered a comfortable and economical alternative in the days before central air conditioning was widely available by allowing cool breezes to enter while shading the house from the intensity of the sun's rays.

Finding the Charm in Charm City

Featuring one of the classic bungalow designs, these painted screens on a house just north of Eastern Avenue near Patterson Park are both attractive and practical. They serve as streetside art for pedestrians to view, but, more importantly, they provide privacy for the homeowner because they prevent people from being able to look inside.

The wire-mesh windowscreen dates to 1861, when it was developed to keep flies, mosquitoes, and other insects out of a building. The Victorians first painted screens with typically somber designs, and some companies used painted screens for advertising. The Baltimore folk art tradition was started in 1914 by William Anton Octavek when he painted the screen doors on his grocery store with images of meats and vegetables. He could then let the air in while keeping the sun out. Having worked early in his adult life as a demonstrator of the Brookmonde spraypaint airbrush, Octavek had some art training. When a coworker complained of the lack of privacy because of the open window by her desk, he painted a vase of flowers and a curtain on the outside of the screen, thereby preventing people from looking in and distracting her.

The use of painted screens was quickly adopted in the East Baltimore neighborhoods where the Italian, Polish, and Eastern European immigrants took meticulous care of their homes and neighborhoods. This custom-made art form provided an attractive means of allowing privacy while living in a confined space.

William Octavek painted screens for forty years and generously passed on his knowledge of the craft to others. Today these painted screens are still being produced, and they are as much a trademark of the city as are the marble steps.

Even though its front steps still advertise "Hot French Fry's," this corner building near the west side of Patterson Park serves today as a private residence. But it was typical of the corner grocery stores, restaurants, and shops that were among the many "Mom and Pop" businesses so common in city neighborhoods. Utilizing the ever familiar red brick, stained glass window, and white marble steps, it continues to represent the rich heritage of earlier years, when many street corners had similar places to visit.

The journey ends on a quiet street near Patterson Park with this most classic symbol of Baltimore. During the early 1800s, when much of the center of the city was being built, the genuine white marble found at the Beaver Dam quarry in the Cockeysville area north of the city was convenient, plentiful, inexpensive, and permanent. It also provided a pleasing contrast to the red brick that was commonly used in the construction of these buildings.

For more than a hundred years, stonecutters carved the genuine white marble from the quarry and used it for countless sets of steps in the city. On an 1827 tour of America, the mother of the English novelist Anthony Trollope remarked on the abundance of white marble with which the city's houses were adorned.

When the Beaver Dam quarry was closed in 1934, marble from other local and out-of-state quarries was used to fill the demand for the tradition that had become a mark of respectability. In many neighborhoods, a visitor can still witness the daily tradition of scrubbing these steps in order to maintain their sparkling beauty.

About Polaroid Image Transfers

Polaroid image transfers look like no other photographic medium. They have been described as "frescolike," they can look much like watercolor paintings, and they are often subtle, moody, and timeless in appearance. Their colors are usually soft and warm, but they can also convey vivid, luminous color of a very different quality than conventional photographic color materials offer.

Polaroid transfers are most often made using Polaroid type 59 4″ × 5″ instant color film. They can be made "live" by exposing the Polaroid film directly in a 4″ × 5″ view camera, then processing the transfer on the spot immediately after exposure. They can also be made by projecting transparency materials (such as color slides) directly onto the film in the darkroom by means of a color photographic enlarger. If the second method is used, multiples of the same image can more easily be made.

A primary quality of image transfers is that no two are ever exactly alike. This is the result of subtle variations of paper, time, temperature, and texture, thereby ensuring that the original transfer is truly "one of a kind." The Polaroid transfers for this book were made on 100 percent acid-free watercolor paper. Occasionally, professional quality watercolors or colored pencil were added to enhance an image. As with any valued original art work, image transfers should not be displayed in strong or direct light for long periods of time.

About the Photographer

Huguette Despault May was born in Ottawa, Ontario, and grew up in Toledo, Ohio. Her art and photography studies began at the Ontario College of Art in 1971 and included further study in painting, illustration, and photography at various schools in the United States.

While she specialized in pastel portraiture and still life, her early career centered on illustration and commissioned works in a wide range of fine art media. During this time, Huguette's work received numerous awards in national juried competitions and invitational exhibitions. She has served as president of the Maryland Pastel Society and has been a juried member of the Pastel Society of America.

In 1990 she established her own professional photography service, Art & Image, at first specializing in the photography of artwork and sculpture and later expanding to include the electronic restoration and retouching of photographs. She became the first Maryland member of the Professional Photographers of America Inc. to become a certified electronic imager.

Huguette and her husband, Tom, lived in Baltimore for eleven years until 1996, when they moved to eastern Massachusetts.

About the Author

Anthea Smith is an award-winning painter who also writes. Her curiosity for the world around her was nurtured by a childhood spent traveling as a dependent in the U.S. Air Force, when she lived in various spots from Albuquerque, New Mexico, to Cambridge, England, and many places in between.

Her early professional experiences include work as a graphic artist, a production manager, and the vice president of an advertising agency in Baltimore. After moving to southwest Arkansas in 1976, she worked as a copywriter at a local radio station. When she returned to Baltimore she attended the Maryland Institute, College of Art, earning a Certificate in Fine Arts in Painting in 1987.

Anthea lives in the mill neighborhood of Hampden with her husband, Bert (author of the book *Greetings from Baltimore: Postcard Views of the City*, also available from Johns Hopkins), and four cats.

Library of Congress Cataloging-in-Publication Data

May, Huguette D.
    Finding the charm in charm city : affectionate views of Baltimore / photographs by
Huguette D. May ; text by Anthea Smith; with a foreword by Michael Olesker.
        p.   cm.
    ISBN 0-8018-5929-8 (alk. paper)
    1. Baltimore (Md.)—Pictorial works.   2. Roads—Maryland—Baltimore—Pictorial
works.   3. Baltimore (Md.)—Buildings, structures, etc.—Pictorial works.   I. Smith,
Anthea, 1947- .   II. Title.
F189.B143M39   1998
975.2′6—dc21   98-11466
                                                                                              CIP